A GLOSSARY OF
HISTORICAL LINGUISTICS

A Glossary of
Historical Linguistics

*Lyle Campbell and
Mauricio J. Mixco*

The University of Utah Press
Salt Lake City

© 2007 by Lyle Campbell and Mauricio J. Mixco

First published in the UK by Edinburgh University Press Ltd

Published in North America by The University of Utah Press

Typeset in Sabon
by Norman Tilley Graphics Ltd, Northampton,
and printed and bound in Great Britain
by Cox & Wyman Ltd, Reading

Library of Congress Cataloging-in-Publication Data

Campbell, Lyle.
 A glossary of historical linguistics / Lyle Campbell and Mauricio J. Mixco.
   p. cm.
  ISBN-13: 978-0-87480-892-6 (cloth : alk. paper)
  ISBN-13: 978-0-87480-893-3 (pbk. : alk. paper)
  1. Historical linguistics–Terminology.
  I. Mixco, Mauricio J. II. Title.
  P140.C359 2007
  417'.703–dc22

                                    2006031649

Contents

Note to the Reader

Throughout the book italics are used for emphasis, to highlight words and phrases that are important, but that are not themselves key words found in entries in this glossary. Most such terms are straightforward and the notions they represent are covered elsewhere in the volume under more direct or conventional terms.

abductive change   Language change due to **abduction**.

abduction   From American philosopher Charles S. Peirce, a reasoned guess about how an observed fact may have come about; reasoning from an effect to its cause; a kind of reasoning aimed at coming up with good hypotheses to explain observed cases; reasoning where, from a specific instance, a general conclusion is drawn, thought to be relevant to other similar cases, though this may not in fact be the case; thus, when applied to language, it can lead to language change. Introduced into linguistics by Henning Andersen (1973) and Raimo Anttila (1972).

aberrancy   see **shared aberrancy**

Abkhaz-Adyge   More commonly called **Northwest Caucasian**

ablaut (also sometimes called **apophony, vowel gradation** and **vowel grades**)   An alternation of vowels in the same root (or etymologically related words) that correlates with meaning differences. Ablaut is a characteristic particularly of **Indo-European** languages, especially the older ones such as Sanskrit, Greek, Latin and Germanic, though the term is also used for vowel alternations in grammatically related forms in other languages. The irregular ('strong') verbs of English illustrate ablaut alternations, for example *sing/sang/sung, bring/brought/ brought, seek/sought/sought, break/broke/broken, drive/ drove/driven.* In Indo-European linguistics it is common to speak of *e-grade* (with /e/) and *o-grade* (with /o/) ablaut. The distinction between /e/ and /o/, and between /ē/ and /ō/, is labeled *qualitative ablaut*, while the distinction between /e/, /ē/, and Ø ('zero') and between /o/, /ō/, and Ø is called *quantitative ablaut*. With /e/ or /o/, the root is said to be in *full grade*; when the vowel is gone (Ø), it is in *zero grade. Qualitative ablaut* is exemplified in Classical Greek *pét-o-mai* 'fly' (*e-grade*), *pot-ē* 'flight' (*o-grade*), *e-pt-omēn* 'flew' (*zero-grade*). *Quantitative ablaut* is illustrated in the second vowel of Classical Greek *patér-es* 'fathers' (nominative plural) (*full grade*), *patēr* 'father' (nominative singular), *patr-ós* 'father's' (genitive singular) (*zero grade*).

The ablaut alternations are thought to have been conditioned by the position of the stress in **Proto-Indo-European**; however, later linguistic changes in most Indo-European languages have obscured the probable earlier phonological conditioning, so that the ablaut alternations become part of the morphology of the languages. Similar vowel alternations in non-Indo-European languages are also sometimes called *ablaut* as are consonantal alternations in morphologically related words (as in **Yuman, Siouan** and other North American Indian language families).

absolute chronology   The assignment of linguistic events to a specific date in the past. Absolute chronology for linguistic events usually depends on correlations of linguistic facts with information about dating from outside of linguistics. For example, when linguistic forms are found in written material, conclusions that the linguistic form must predate the time of the writing are safe. See also **chronology, relative chronology.**

accent   see **dialect**

accommodation   The process by which speakers of different languages or varieties of a single language alter their speech to be more similar to the pronunciation and structure of the language of people with whom the speak, thereby *accommodating* to their form of language.

accommodation (of loanwords)   see **naturalization**

accretion zone (formerly also called a **residual zone**)   An area where genetic and structural diversity of languages are high and increase over time through immigration. Examples are the Caucasus, the Himalayas, the Ethiopian highlands and the northern Rift Valley, California, the Pacific Northwest of North America, Amazonia, northern Australia and New Guinea (Nichols 1997: 369).

acculturation   see **linguistic acculturation, language contact**

acronym   A word derived from the initial letters of each of the successive parts of a compound term or successive words, for example *UNESCO* [yunéskow] from *United Nations Educational, Scientific and Cultural Organization*; *emcee* from 'master of ceremonies'; *radar* from 'radio direction and ranging'; *scuba* (diving) from 'self contained underwater breathing apparatus'; and *Gestapo* from German *Geheime Staatspolizei* 'secret state's police'. Acronym also refers to abbreviations where the letters are spelled out: *ASAP* 'as soon as possible', *CD* 'compact disc', *DJ* 'disc jockey', *UK*, *USA* and *VCR* from 'video cassette recorder'.

actualization   see **extension, realization**

actuation problem   Concern with explaining why a given linguistic change occurs at the particular time and place that it does, with how changes begin and proceed and with what starts a change and what carries it along. See also **Weinreich–Labov–Herzog model of language change.**

adstratum (also called **adstrate language**)   In language contact, a language that influences a neighboring language or languages. Often it is assumed the language has relatively equal prestige with those it influences, as is the case, for example, with Chukchi, which, though they are of equal status, has influenced Siberian Yupik (de Reuse 1994). If a language has greater status it is typically called a **superstratum** (**superstrate** language), and if it has less status it is usually referred to as a **substratum** (**substrate** language). See also **areal linguistics, borrowing, language contact, substratum, superstratum.**

affective symbolism   see **sound symbolism**

affrication   The change in which some sound becomes an affricate (a speech sound with multiple articulatory gestures, beginning with a stop that is released into a fricative); for example, in the **Second Germanic Consonant Shift** the stops /p, t, k/ became affricates (pf, ts, kx), respectively (as in High German, p > pf in *Pfad* 'path', t > ts in *Zunge* 'tongue' [where German 'z' = /ts/] and *acht* 'eight' [where German 'ch' = /x/ – from former

/kx/]). The term affrication is also applied to synchronic rules of phonology that produce affricates.

Afroasiatic, Afro-Asiatic (sometimes also called **Afrasian**; older related names [not necessarily involving all the Afroasiatic groups] include: **Hamito-Semitic**, Erythraic and Lisramic)   A hypothesis of genetic relationship that includes: **Semitic, Berber,** *Egyptian,* **Cushitic, Omotic** and **Chadic** – some 370 languages, with about 150 in Chadic alone and not including some fifty extinct varieties of Semitic. Afroasiatic enjoys wide support among linguists, but it is not uncontroversial, especially with regard to which of the groups assumed to be genetically related to one another are to be considered true members of the **phylum**. There is disagreement concerning Cushitic, and Omotic (formerly called Sidama or West Cushitic) is disputed; the great linguistic diversity within Omotic makes it a questionable entity for some. Chadic is held to be uncertain by others. **Typological** and **areal** problems contribute to these doubts. For example, some treat Cushitic and Omotic together as a **linguistic area (Sprachbund)** of seven families within Afroasiatic. Some believe there is a closer connection between Berber, Semitic and either Egyptian or Cushitic than among the other groups in Greenberg's (1963) Afroasiatic classification, though it is not certain yet whether this is indeed a closer genetic subgroup or whether these three merely share more diffused areal features.

agglutinating, agglutinative   In language typology, the type of language characterized by **agglutination**, the addition of affixes to roots (often several affixes) where the addition causes no significant phonological changes in the root and the different affixes are readily identifiable and easily segmented from the root and from one another.

Some languages that exemplify this type are Japanese, Mongolian, Shoshone and Turkish.

agglutination The process in which affixes are added to roots; in another sense, the **amalgamation** of two or more independent words into a single word, for example, *nevertheless* from *never* + *the* + *less*. Some early views, sometimes referred to as 'agglutination theory', held that languages started out with only independent words, and through agglutination some of these words were attached to others and in the process became grammatical affixes of various sorts, and eventually, through **sound change** and **analogy**, produced the various structural types known in the languages of the world. See **amalgamation, isolating language, synthetic languages.** See also **agglutinating, agglutinative.**

Algic A large North American language family with widely spread representatives from the Pacific coast of California to the Atlantic seaboard, from Labrador to South Carolina and northern Mexico. It is made up of the large and widespread **Algonquian** subfamily and *Ritwan*, which contains Wiyot and Yurok of northern California. Algic was first proposed by Sapir (1913) and remained controversial for a considerable time, but was demonstrated conclusively by Mary R. Haas (1958a) to the satisfaction of all.

Algonkian-Gulf A **distant genetic relationship** proposed by Mary R. Haas (1958b, 1960) linking **Algonquian** and her hypothesized 'Gulf' languages. She later doubted Gulf. and, consequently, Algonkian-Gulf has no support among specialists today.

Algonquian (sometimes spelled Algonkian) A large, well-known **language family** of some twenty-seven languages spread from the Rockies (Alberta, Montana, Wyoming) to the East Coast (Labrador to the Carolinas). Algonquian is a branch of the broader **Algic** family, which includes **Ritwan** (Wiyot and Yurik of California).

Almosan-Keresiouan Very large-scale hypothesis of **distant genetic relationship** proposed by Joseph H. Greenberg (1987), a division of his now rejected **Amerind hypothesis**. In the hypothesis, Almosan-Keresiouan consists of two large groups, **Almosan** (which combines **Algic** and **Mosan**) and **Keresiouan** (combining **Keresan** and **Siouan**). Almosan-Keresiouan has no support among specialists today.

Altaic hypothesis A hypothesis of **distant genetic relationship** taking its name from the Altai mountains of central Asia; it holds that **Turkic**, **Mongolian** and **Tungusic** (Manchu-Tungusic), together comprising some forty languages, are genetically related. More extended versions of the Altaic hypothesis would include **Korean** and **Japanese**, sometimes also *Ainu*. Various scholars in the early and mid 1800s proposed classifications that would group some or all of the 'Altaic' languages together, but typically these were included in larger, more poorly defined proposed affiliations, such as the now abandoned **Ural-Altaic hypothesis**. While 'Altaic' is repeated in encyclopedias and handbooks most specialists in these languages no longer believe that the three traditional supposed Altaic groups, Turkic, Mongolian and Tungusic, are related. In spite of this, Altaic does have a few dedicated followers.

The most serious problems for the Altaic proposal are the extensive lexical borrowing across inner Asia and among the 'Altaic' languages, lack of significant numbers of convincing cognates, extensive areal diffusion and typologically commonplace traits presented as evidence of relationship. The shared 'Altaic' traits typically cited include vowel harmony, relatively simple phoneme inventories, **agglutination**, their exclusively suffixing nature, (S)OV ([Subject]-Object-Verb) word order and the fact that their non-main clauses are mostly non-finite (participial) constructions. These shared features are not only commonplace typological traits that occur with frequency in unrelated languages of the world and therefore could easily have developed independently, but they are also areal traits, shared by a number of languages in surrounding regions the structural properties of which were not well-known when the hypothesis was first framed. The hypothesis, in spite of its long history, has been controversial almost from its beginning.

amalgamation (sometimes also misleadingly referred to as **agglutination**)   The fusion of two or more words occurring in a phrase into a single word with a more idiomatic meaning; for example, English *never the less* > *nevertheless*; German *nicht desto weniger* > *nichtdestoweniger* 'nonetheless'; Spanish *tan poco* > *tampoco* 'neither'.

Amazonian linguistic area   A proposed **linguistic area** that covers the languages of the vast Amazon basin of South America (around 4 million square miles), including language from the following families: **Arawakan** (**Maipurean**), *Arawan*, **Cariban**, *Chapacuran*, **Gê(an)**, *Panoan*, *Puinavean*, *Tacanan*, *Tucanoan* and *Tupian*. Among other traits shared across these language families are: (1) an Object-before-Subject word order (VOS [Verb-Object-Subject], OVS [Object-Verb-Subject], OSV [Object-Subject-Verb]); (2) subject and object agreement on verb with no free pronouns; (3) nominalization rather than clause subordination; (4) nominal modifiers following heads; (5) no agentive passives; (6) rarity of indirect speech constructions; (7) lack of coordinating conjunctions; (8) ergativity; (9) very complex verbal morphology; (10) noun classifiers or gender systems; (11) possessive constructions with the order Possessor Possessed (as in 'the man his-canoe'); (12) prefixes, few suffixes; (13) a very small number of lexical numbers (typically with only one, two, often also three, sometimes up to four, not more). (Derbyshire and Payne 1990, Derbyshire and Pullum 1986, Dixon and Aikhenvald 1999: 8–10; compare Campbell 1997: 348–50.)

amelioration   see **elevation**

Amerind hypothesis   Based on his much criticized method of **multilateral comparison**, Joseph Greenberg's (1987) proposal of **distant genetic relationship** in which he held that all Native American languages, except 'Na-Dené' and **Eskimo-Aleut**, belong to a single, very large 'Amerind' genetic grouping. The Amerind hypothesis is rejected by nearly all practicing American Indianists and by most historical linguists. Specialists maintain that valid methods do not at present permit classification of Native American languages into fewer than about 180 independent **language families** and **isolates**.

Amerind has been highly criticized on various grounds. There is an excessive number of errors in Greenberg's data. Where Greenberg stops – after assembling superficial similarities and declaring them due to common ancestry – is where other linguists begin. Since such similarities can be due to **chance similarity, borrowing, onomatopoeia, sound symbolism, nursery words** (the *mama, papa, nana, dada, caca* sort), misanalysis and much more, for a plausible proposal of remote linguistic relationship one must attempt to eliminate all other possible explanations, leaving a shared common ancestor as the most likely. Greenberg made no attempt to eliminate these other explanations, and the similarities he amassed appear to be due mostly to accident and a combination of these other factors. In various instances, Greenberg compared arbitrary segments of words, equated words with very different meanings (for example, 'excrement/night/grass'), misidentified many languages, failed to analyze the morphology of some words and falsely analyzed that of others, neglected regular sound correspondences, failed to eliminate loanwords and misinterpreted well-established findings. The Amerind 'etymologies' proposed are often limited to a very few languages of the many involved. (See Adelaar 1989; Campbell 1988, 1997; Kimball 1992; McMahon and McMahon 1995; Poser 1992; Rankin 1992; Ringe 1992, 1996.) Finnish, Japanese, Basque and other randomly chosen languages fit Greenberg's Amerind data as well as or better than do any of the American Indian languages in his 'etymologies'; Greenberg's method has proven incapable of distinguishing implausible relationships from Amerind generally. In short, it is with good reason Amerind has been rejected. See also **multilateral comparison**.

analogical extension   In analogical change extension of the already existing alternation of some pattern to new forms that did not formerly undergo the alternation; for example, *dived* was replaced by *dove* in the speech of many on analogy with the verb pattern in *drive/drove*, *ride/rode* etc. See also **analogy**.

analogical leveling Reduces the number of variants a form has; it makes paradigms more uniform. Forms that formerly underwent alternations no longer do so after analogical leveling. For example, the earlier 'comparative' and 'superlative' forms of *old* have been leveled from the pattern *old/elder/eldest* to the non-alternating pattern *old/older/oldest* (and now the words *elder* and *eldest* remain only in restricted contexts, not as the regular 'comparative' and 'superlative' of *old*). See also **analogy**.

analogy A process whereby one form of a language becomes more like another with which it is somehow associated; that is, analogical change involves a relation of similarity in which one piece of a language changes to become more like another pattern in that language when speakers perceive the changing part as similar to the pattern which it changes to become like. For example, earlier English *brethren* 'brothers' changed to *brothers*, with *brother/brothers* coming in line with the pattern of many nouns that have *-s* plurals as in *sister/sisters*, *mother/mothers*, *son/sons* etc.

analytic Term to characterize constructions that employ independent words rather than bound morphemes to express grammatical relationships. Thus, Spanish *voy a comer* 'I am going to eat, I will eat' is the analytic future, expressed by independent words, while *comeré* 'I will eat' is not, since the first person future marker *-ré* is a bound morpheme. In language typology, an *analytic language* is one characterized by a predominance of such analytic constructions and relative lack of bound morphology. See also **isolating language**.

analytic language see **analytic**

analyzability of words   In *Wörter und Sachen*, the more opaque a word is morphologically – when it has no detectable morphological analysis – the longer it can be presumed to have been in a language. Or, put differently, words with no discernible morphological analysis can be assumed to be older in the language than words that do have a clear morphological analysis. This can be a useful tool in reconstructing prehistory based on linguistic evidence. The analyzability criterion can also be applied to place names, for which it is assumed that the non-analyzable (monomorphemic) names, such as *York*, *London*, are older, while names, such as *New York*, *New Jersey* are younger. This provides a potential chronology for a language's occupation of a given territory based on whether place names appear older because they are not analyzable into multiple morphemes. The longer the occupation, the more abundant the opaque toponyms; more recent occupation is reflected in relatively more transparent, analyzable ones. Sometimes also called **tractability**. See also *Wörter und Sachen*.

anaptyxis (< Greek 'unfolding')   A type of **epenthesis** in which a vowel is inserted between two consonants; this is often thought to be motivated by a tendency towards greater ease of pronunciation. Examples from dialects of English are: *athlete* as '*athullete*' or *film* as '*filum*'. Anaptyctic vowels are also called *parasitic* or *parasite* vowels, and, in Sanskrit *svarabhakti vowels*, from the Hindu grammarian tradition.

Anatolian   A branch of **Indo-European**; the Anatolian subfamily includes **Hittite**, Lydian, Palaic, Luvian, Lycian and Carian, ancient extinct languages once spoken in Asia Minor. Anatolian is generally considered to be the first branch to have split off from other Indo-

European languages. See also **Indo-Hittite hypothesis**.

Andaman languages, Andamanese   Several **languages** of the Andaman Islands (on the west of the Bay of Bengal), ten languages of the Great Andaman group and three of the Little Andaman group. It has so far proven impossible to demonstrate a genetic relationship among these distinct Andaman languages. Greenberg (1971) proposed that Andaman languages belong to his mostly rejected **Indo-Pacific** hypothesis, though the evidence does not sustain such a hypothesis.

aphaeresis (< Greek *apo-* 'away' + *hairein* 'to take')   A **sound change** in which a word-initial vowel is lost, as in the occasional pronunciation of *American* as '*merican*'. A broader sense of the term sometimes includes **loss** of any initial sound, including consonants, as in the loss of the initial *k* of English *knee*, *knife* etc. In a less technical sense, aphaeresis is the loss of one or more sounds from the beginning of a word, as in *till* for *until*. Spanish **loanwords** in the indigenous languages of the American Southwest evince such examples in their **borrowing** of the word *American*: Ute *míríká*, Hopi *velakáána*, Zuni *meliká*, Acoma *merigáánu* (compare Navajo *belagáána*; Towa *belegaaní*, New Mexico Tewa *merikanu/beliganu*).

apocope (< Greek *apo-* 'away' + *koptein* 'to cut')   A **sound change** in which a word-final vowel is lost. A broader sense sometimes includes **loss** of any final sound, including consonants. For example, the final *e* after certain sounds was regularly deleted – apocopated – in Spanish, as in *pane* > *pan* 'bread', *sole* > *sol* 'sun' etc.

apparent merger   see **near merger**

apparent-time study In sociolinguistic research dealing with on-going changes, a **variable** (a linguistic trait subject to social or stylistic variation) is investigated at one particular point in time. To the extent that the variation correlates with age it is assumed that a **change in progress** is under way and that the variant most characteristic of older speakers' speech represents the earlier stage and the variant more typical of younger speakers' speech shows what it is changing to. The age-gradient distribution shows the change in progress. An example of this sort is the on-going merger of diphthongs /iə/ (as in *ear*, *cheer*) and /ɛə/ (as in *air*, *chair*) in New Zealand English, where, in general, older speakers maintain the contrast more, but, increasingly, younger speakers merge the two to /iə/ (see Gordon et al. 2004). See also **change in progress, real-time study**.

Appendix Probi Latin for *Probus's appendix*, compiled in the third to fourth centuries AD to assist speakers of the emergent **Romance** or vernacular Latin not only to spell words correctly but also, more interestingly, to avoid stigmatized vernacular pronunciations. The appendix is arranged in two columns, with the 'proper' form on the left and the stigmatized form on the right: *x not y*, for example, *oculus non oclus*, that is, *oculus* not *oclus* for 'eye'. For the modern student, the latter is an invaluable and scarce record of usage prevalent in Probus's time and an indication of changes the language was undergoing.

applied historical linguistics see **linguistic prehistory**

Arawakan A large South American **language family** with representatives spread from Central America to Argentina, comprising some sixty-five **languages**, of which over thirty are extinct. Some scholars prefer **Maipurean**

(or **Maipuran**) as the name of the family of languages known to be related, reserving **Arawakan** as the name for a possibly broader **phylum** that would include the known Arawakan/Maipurean languages as well, possibly, as some other languages and language families not yet clearly demonstrated as belonging to the family.

archaism (sometimes also **relic, retention** and, less often, **plesiomorphy**)   A form or construction characteristic of a past form of a **language**, a vestige, that survives chiefly in specialized uses. Archaisms are now exceptional or marginal to the languages in which they are found; they are most commonly preserved in special kinds of language such as in proverbs, folk poetry, folk ballads, legal documents, prayers and religious texts, very formal genres or stylistic variants. For example, English *pease* for 'pea', is an archaism preserved in the nursery rhyme 'pease porridge hot, pease porridge cold, pease porridge in the pot nine days old'; it reflects older *pease* 'pea' before it was changed by analogical **back formation** to *pea*. In the Spanish of northern New Mexico and southern Colorado, as in many other non-standard dialects, certain lexical items, morphological forms and pronunciations have been preserved that are no longer in common use in Standard Spanish. Thus, the Modern Standard Spanish preterite form of *traer* 'to bring', is *traje* [tráxe] 'I brought', whereas the northern New Mexican archaism preserves the etymologically more faithful forms: *truje* [trúxe] 'I brought' from Ibero-Romance *trauxe* ~ *trouxe* [tráuše ~ tróuše] < Latin *traxui* [tráksui] 'I brought' (compare Portuguese *trouxe* [tróušə ~ tróuši]). Similarly, Modern Standard Spanish has *ví* 'I saw', while New Mexican Spanish preserves the archaism *vide* 'I saw' (< Latin *vidi* 'I saw'). Examples of archaisms involving English grammar include the verb forms with *-eth* 'third person' (*he maketh*) and *-st* 'second person' agreement (*thou annointest*), the auxiliary forms *hath, hast, art, doth* (*doeth*), and the archaic second singular pronoun forms, *thou, thee, thy, thine*.

areal linguistics   Concerned with the diffusion of structural features across language boundaries within a geographical region, called a **linguistic area**, where because of **language contact** and **borrowing**, languages of a region come to share certain structural features – not only borrowed words but also shared elements of sound and grammar.

articulatory space   see **maximum differentiation**

assibilation   A change in which a sound (or sequence of sounds) becomes a sibilant. For example, the change of Latin /k/ before front vowels in various **Romance** languages illustrates assibilation, as in the change of *centum* /kentum/ 'hundred' to Italian *cento* /tʃento/, Spanish *ciento* /syento ~ θyento/, French *cent* /sã/. Assibilation can be a **synchronic** or a **diachronic** process.

assimilation   A change in which one sound becomes more similar to another through the influence of a neighboring, usually adjacent, sound. Assimilatory changes are often subclassified in terms of *total-partial, contact-distant* and *regressive-progressive* dichotomies. A change is **total** assimilation if a sound becomes identical to another by taking on all of its phonetic features. The change is *partial* if the assimilating sound acquires some traits of another, but does not become fully identical to it. A *regressive* (also called *anticipatory*) change is one in which the sound that undergoes the change comes earlier in the word (nearer the beginning) than the sound that causes or conditions the assimilation. *Progressive* assimilation affects sounds that come later in the word (closer to the end) than the conditioning sound. Some examples of these kinds of assimilation follow: *Total contact regressive assimilation*: change of Latin *octo* to Italian *otto* 'eight', *noctem* to *notte* 'night'. *Total contact progressive assimilation*: Proto-Germanic **hulnis* to Old English *hyll* (Modern English *hill*) 'hill'. *Partial contact regressive assimilation*: the assimilation of nasals to the point of articulation of following sounds, illustrated in English by the changes in the prefix /In-/ 'not', as in *in-possible* > *impossible*; *in-tolerant* > *intolelrant*; *in-compatible* > *iŋcompatible* (in the last case, the change of *n* to *ŋ* is optional). *Partial contact progressive assimilation*: English suffixes spelled with -*s* assimilated, becoming voiced, after a preceding voiced (non-sibilant) consonant, as in /dɔgz/ 'dogs', /rIbz/ 'ribs' (though remained voiceless with preceding voiceless sounds, as in /kæts/ 'cats'. *Distant* (non-adjacent) *assimilation*: Proto-Indo-European **penkʷe* > Latin *kʷinkʷe* (spelled *quinque*) *'five'* (*total distant regressive assimilation*).

In *mutual assimilation*, segments affect each other, with change in both the preceding and following sound, as in the change from Latin *rapidum* 'devouring', which lost its medial vowel, *rapdu*, and then underwent mutual assimilation to become Italian *ratto* 'kidnapping'.

Athabaskan A large North American **language family** (actually a subfamily of **Eyak–Athabaskan**) spread from Alaska to Mexico, whose some forty member languages include Navajo and several Apache languages. Eyak of Alaska is a sister to Athabaskan, in the larger **Eyak–Athabaskan** family. Sometimes spelled Athapaskan, Athapascan, Athabascan.

attestation (also sometimes called *documentation*, also **witness**). For a given linguistic form, the evidence that the form is or was clearly found in the language in question. Often though not exclusively, attestation is said of written evidence of the existence of some linguistic form in an earlier stage of the language involved. For example, we say, English *gal* (variant of *girl*) was first attested in 1785 – occurred in the oldest known written source to contain the word.

Australian, Proto-Australian   A hypothesis that all of the twenty-eight **language families** in Australia may ultimately be genetically related and belong to one large **macro-family**. Many Australian linguists are sympathetic to the possibility that all the Australian languages may descend from a single common ancestor; however, the evidence is limited and does not eliminate other possible explanations. Given that humans have been in Australia for about 50,000 years, even if there had then been an original Proto-Australian, so much change would have taken place in its descendants that it would probably be impossible, using standard linguistic techniques such as the **comparative method**, to demonstrate they all share a common ancestry so far back in time.

Austric   A proposed **distant genetic relationship** that would group **Austroasiatic** and **Austronesian**. The hypothesis is mostly doubted, but has some supporters. It was first proposed by Wilhelm Schmidt (1906).

Austroasiatic, Austro-Asiatic   A proposed **genetic relationship** between **Mon-Khmer** and **Munda**, accepted as valid by many scholars but not by all.

Austronesian   The world's largest **language family** both in terms of the number of languages – approximately 1,200 – and, spreading from Taiwan to New Zealand and Hawaii, and from Madagascar to Easter Island, in its geographical area. There are about 270 million speakers of Austronesian languages. The full extent of the family and a relative consensus concerning its subgrouping has emerged only since the 1970s. Earlier, it was often called *Malayo-Polynesian*, though not all the subgroups were then recognized, in particular not the more distant relatives in Taiwan. Most scholars today see Proto-Austronesian as having split up between 5,000 and 6,000 years ago into 'Formosan' and 'Malayo-Polynesian'. It is not certain whether the Formosan languages (some ten indigenous Austronesian languages spoken in Taiwan) constitute a single branch or several distinct branches of the Austronesian family tree, perhaps dividing into Atayalic (northern), Tsouic (central) and Paiwanic (southern) groups. Taiwan or perhaps the South China coastal mainland is generally thought to be the area of the Proto-Austronesian homeland. Malayo-Polynesian (MP) is a clear subgroup; it branches into Western MP and Central/Eastern MP, which then divides into Central MP (including languages of the Lesser Sundas, Maluku and coastal regions of Irian Jaya) and Eastern MP – these three, Western MP, Central MP and Eastern MP, are less secure groupings; Western MP, which includes all the Philippine languages as well as languages of Sumatra, Java, Madura, Bali, Lombok and parts of Kalimantan (Borneo), plus Austronesian languages of the Malay Peninsula, Chamic languages (spoken by ethnic minorities in Vietnam and Cambodia), Malagasy (Madagascar), Chamorro and Palau, is controversial. Eastern MP split into two branches: South Halmahera–West New Guinea and Oceanic. The very large Oceanic group, with some 500 languages, includes Polynesian, Rotuman, Fijian; Northern New Guinea, Papuan Tip, Meso-Melanesian; Admiralties; Southeast Solomonic; Nuclear Micronesian; Central–North Vanuatu; and New Caledonia–Loyalties. There are some 220 Oceanic languages in Papua New Guinea alone.

Austro-Tai A mostly discounted hypothesis of distant genetic relationship proposed by Paul Benedict that would group together the **Austronesian, Tai-Kadai** and **Miao-Yao.** (Benedict 1975, 1990.)

avoidance of homophony Any change in which homophony (words with different meaning sounding the same) is avoided or eliminated. Avoidance of homophony can take several forms. The most often cited cases involve *lexical replacement* or *lexical loss*, as in the famous example from Gascony where original *ll* changed to *t*, so that *gal* 'rooster' (from *gallus*) would have become *gat*, leaving *gat* 'rooster' homophonous with *gat* 'cat'. This homophony was avoided by the replacement of 'rooster' with other words originally meaning 'pheasant' or 'vicar', allowing 'cat' and 'rooster' to be distinguished. Some argue that *prevention* or blocking of sound changes, takes place in some instances to avoid homophony. For example, in some German dialects sound changes (loss of -g- and the unrounding of *ü*) would have left *liegen* [liːgən] 'to lie (down)' and *lügen* [lyːgən] 'to lie (tell falsehoods)' homophonous, but these otherwise regular sound changes were blocked in these words to preserve the distinction between these two common words. In *deflection*, homophonies are avoided by irregular or spontaneous changes that maintain a distinction between the clashing forms. For example, Middle

English *cony*, *coney* or *cunny* 'rabbit' was considered too close in pronunciation to a phonetically similar obscenity and so was changed by deflection to *bunny*.

Aymaran (also sometimes called **Jaqi, Aru**) A small **language family** of the Andes region, containing the large Aymara language, which has about 1.5 million speakers, plus two smaller ones, Jaqaru and Kawki.

Aztec–Tanoan A proposed **distant genetic relationship** that would group **Uto–Aztecan** and **Kiowa–Tanoan**, now mostly abandoned. (Whorf and Trager 1937; Miller 1959, Campbell 1997: 269–73.)

B

babbling word see **nursery word**

back formation A type of **folk etymology** in which a word is assumed to have a morphological composition that it did not originally have, usually a root plus some affix, so that when the assumed but historically inaccurate affix is removed, a new root is created, as in *pea* < *pease*, *cherry* < *cherise* (thought to have had a plural 's'); *edit* < *editor*, *sculpt* < *sculptor* (thought to have had the *-or* or *-er* suffix of someone who performs the action of a verb). Sometimes also called **retrograde formation**.

Balkan linguistic area The best known of all **linguistic areas**. The languages of the Balkans linguistic area are Greek, Albanian, Serbo-Croatian, Bulgarian, Macedonian and Rumanian (to which some scholars also add Romani and Turkish). Some salient traits of the Balkans linguistic area are (1) a central vowel /ɨ/ (or /ə/) (not present in Greek or Macedonian); (2) syncretism of dative and genitive cases (dative and genitive merged in form and function); this is illustrated by Rumanian *fetei* 'to the girl' or 'girl's', as in *am data o carte fetei* 'I gave the letter **to the girl**' and *frate fetei* 'the **girl's** brother'; (3) postposed articles (not in Greek); for example, Bulgarian *məʒ-ət* 'the man' / *məʒ* 'man'; (4) a periphrastic future (future signalled by an auxiliary verb corresponding to 'want' or 'have', not in Bulgarian or Macedonian), as in Rumanian *voi fuma* 'I will smoke' (literally 'I want [to] smoke') and *am a cínta* 'I will sing' (literally 'I have sing'); (5) periphrastic perfect (with an auxiliary verb corresponding to 'have'); (6) an absence of infinitives (rather with constructions such as 'I want that I go' for 'I want to go'); (7) the double marking of animate objects by use of a pronoun copy, as in Rumanian *i-am scris lui Ion* 'I wrote to John', literally 'to.him-I wrote him John', and Greek *ton vlépo ton jáni* 'I see John', literally 'him.Acc I see him.Acc John'.

Baltic linguistic area   Includes at its core *(Balto-)Finnic* languages (especially Estonian and Livonian), Baltic languages (**Indo-European**) and Baltic German; however, all of the following have also been included in different treatments of the Baltic linguistic area: Old Prussian (extinct), Lithuanian, Latvian (Baltic, branch of Indo-European); the ten Saami (Lapp) languages, Finnish, Estonian, Livonian, Votian, Vepsian, Karelian and others (of the Finnic branch of Finno-Ugric); High German, Low German, Baltic German, Yiddish (West Germanic); Danish, Swedish, Norwegian (North Germanic); Russian, Belorussian, Ukranian, Polish, Kashubian (Slavic); Romani (Indo-Aryan, branch of Indo-European); and Karaim (Turkic). Shared features among languages of the Baltic area include (1) first-syllable stress; (2) palatalization of consonants; (3) tonal contrasts; (4) partitive case/partitive constructions (to signal partially affected objects, equivalent to, for example, 'I ate (some) apple', in Finnic, Lithuanian, Latvian, Russian, Polish etc.; (5) direct objects in the nominative case in a number of constructions that lack overt subjects (Finnic, Baltic, North Russian); (6) evidential mood ('John works hard [it is said/reported/inferred]': Estonian, Livonian, Latvian, Lithuanian); (7) prepositional verbs (as German *aus-gehen* [out-to.go] 'to go out': German, Livonian, Estonian, Baltic and others; (8) Subject–Verb–Object (SVO) basic word order; (9) agreement of adjectives in number with the nouns that they modify (all languages of the area except Saami languages and Karaim); they also agree in case in all except the Scandinavian languages (which have lost case distinctions for adjectives); they also agree in gender in Baltic, Slavic, Scandinavian and German, Yiddish and some others. (Zeps 1962, Koptjevskaja-Tamm et al. 2001.) See also **areal linguistics**.

Bantu   A very large **language family** of sub-Saharan Africa that is itself a subdivision of the Benue–Niger **subfamily** of the larger **Niger–Congo** family. The word *Bantu* means 'the people', made up of the plural prefix *ba-* and the stem *-ntu* 'person'. There are several hundred Bantu languages spoken by about 120 million speakers in Africa. Swahili alone has more than 30 million first-language speakers. Some other Bantu languages include Kikuyu, Shona, Zulu, Xhosa, Sotho and Lingala.

basic assumptions of the comparative method   The consequences of how **reconstruction** by the **comparative method** is performed and of views of sound change. The basic assumptions of the comparative method are (1) the proto-language was uniform with no dialect (or social) variation; (2) language splits are sudden; (3) after the split up of the proto-language there is no subsequent contact among the related languages; (4) sound change is regular. Assumption number one is counterfactual, since all known languages have regional or social variation and different styles. The comparative method is not against variation, but there is nothing in the method that would allow it to address variation directly. This assumption does no more damage to understanding of the proto-language than do modern reference grammars that concentrate on a language's general structure, typically leaving out consideration of regional, social and stylistic variation. The second and third assumptions are a consequence of the fact that the comparative method addresses directly only that material in the related languages that is inherited from the proto-language and has no means of its own for dealing with borrowings (the results of subsequent contact after the spit up of the languages). Borrowing and language contact are, however, not neglected: other techniques deal with borrowing, and the comparative method can help identify loans. The fourth assumption, the regularity of sound change, is valuable to the comparative method, since knowing that a sound changes in a regular fashion gives us the confidence to reconstruct what the sound was like in the parent language from which it comes. If a sound could change in unconstrained, unpredictable ways, we would not be able to determine from a given sound in a daughter language what it may have been in the parent language, or, looking at a particular sound in the parent language, we could not determine what its reflexes in its daughter languages would be. See also **family tree**.

basic vocabulary   Rarely defined explicitly, but understood intuitively to contain terms for common body parts, close kin, frequently encountered aspects of the natural world and low numbers. It is assumed that basic vocabulary is generally more resistant to borrowing and lexical replacement than other kinds of vocabularly, and hence basic vocabulary has played a significant role in **comparative linguistics**. Other terms for basic vocabulary sometimes seen are *core vocabulary*, 'non-cultural' vocabulary and occasionally in English also the terms from German or French *Kernwortschatz, charakteristische Wörter, vocabulaire de base*.

Basque   A well-known language **isolate** of northern Spain and southern France. It has no known relatives, though numerous proposals with little support have attempted to link it with various language families from other parts of the world.

Berber   A family of some twenty **languages** spoken in northern Africa. Berber is usually believed to be one of the branches of **Afroasiatic**.

bleaching   see **semantic bleaching**

blend   see **blending**

blending (also called **contamination**)   Creation of new words by the combination of parts of two or more existing words, for example *smog* < *smoke* + *fog* ; *brunch* < *breakfast* + *lunch* ; *motel* < *motor* + *hotel* ; *blog* < *web log*.

There are also **syntactic blends**, for example the English construction *I'm friends with him* – a blend based on (a) *I'm a friend with him* and (b) *we are friends*.

borrowing   The process in which a language takes linguistic elements from another language and makes them part of its own. The borrowed elements are typically **loanwords**, but borrowing is not restricted just to lexical items taken from one language into another: any linguistic material – sounds, phonological rules, grammatical morphemes, syntactic patterns, semantic associations, discourse strategies – can be borrowed, that is, can be taken over so as to become part of the borrowing language. See also **loanword, language contact, donor language, recipient language**.

branch   see **subgroup**

breaking   The **diphthongization** of a short vowel in particular contexts, most commonly encountered in Germanic linguistics, for example in the history of Afrikaans, English, Frisian and Scandinavian. For example, Old English underwent the breaking of **i > *io*, **e > eo*, **a > ea* before *l* or *r* followed by a consonant, or before *h*, as in **kald- > ceald* 'cold', **erθe > eorþe* 'earth', **nǣh > nēah* 'near', **sæh > seah* 'saw' (compare Beekes 1995: 275, Hogg 1992: 102–3). See **diphthongization**.

broadening   see **widening, semantic change**

bundle of isoglosses   The coincidence/co-occurrence of several **dialect** isoglosses at the same geographical boundary. Such bundling of **isoglosses** is often used to define the boundary of a dialect (or dialect area). See **isogloss**.

$\boxed{\text{C}}$

calque (also called **loan translation** and **semantic loan**)   A type of **borrowing** that involves the transkfer of the semantic content of a word or expression from one language to another without the borrowing of its phonetic form, for example several languages have a calque based on English *skyscraper*: French *gratte-ciel* ('scrape sky'), Spanish *rascacielos* ('scratch skies'), German *Wolkenkratzer* ('clouds scratcher').

Cariban   A large **language family**, with around 60 languages, of northern South America, the Caribbean and the Amazon region.

causes of change   see **explanation of linguistic change, actuation problem, mechanisms of language change**

Cayuse-Molala (also called **Waiilatpuan**)   A genetic classification no longer believed that linked Cayuse (of Orgeon and Washington) and Molala (of Oregon) in a single assumed family. The evidence for this was later shown to be wrong and the hypothesis was abandoned. (See Campbell 1997: 121.)

center of gravity (diversity) model   see **linguistic homeland**

centum language   Any **Indo-European** language from the branches of the family in which velar stops did not become fricatives or affricates, as they did in the **satem languages**, from which the centum languages are distinguished. The name comes from Latin *centum* 'hundred', since words for 'hundred' illustrate the behavior of the velar stop /k/. Centum languages include those from the Celtic, Italic, Germanic, Hellenic, Italic, Anatolian and Tocharian branches. See **satem language**.

Chadic   A very large **language family** of some 150 languages, spoken south of the Sahara desert in a band across south-central Chad republics, southern Niger, northern Nigeria and northern Cameroon. Chadic is usually classified as a branch of **Afroasiatic**. Hausa is the largest Chadic language, with over 20 million speakers.

chain shift   A series of interrelated **sound changes**. One idea behind the chain shifts is that the sounds of a sound system are integrated into a whole the parts of which are interconnected so that a change in one part of the system can have implications for other parts of the system, which lead to additional change. In this view, sound systems tend to be symmetrical or natural, and those that are not, those which have a 'gap' in the phonemic inventory, tend to change to make them symmetrical/natural (to fill in the gap). However, a change that fills one gap may create other gaps elsewhere in the system that then lead to other changes towards symmetry/naturalness to rectify the effects, setting off a chain reaction.

There are two types of chain shifts: **pull chains** (often called **drag chains**) and **push chains**. In a **pull chain**, one change may create a hole in the phonemic pattern (an asymmetry, a gap) that is followed by another change that fills the hole by 'pulling' in some other sound from the system so that it fills the gap; if the sound that shifted to fill the original hole in the pattern leaves a new hole of its own elsewhere in the pattern then another change may 'pull' some other sound in to fill that gap in a chain of interrelated changes.

Behind a **push chain** is the notion that differences between sounds in phonemic systems tend to be maintained to preserve meaning differences of words that otherwise would come to sound alike. In this view, if a sound starts moving into the articulatory space of another sound, this can cause a change whereby the crowded sound moves away from the encroaching sound in order to maintain distinctions. If the fleeing sound is pushed towards the articulatory space of some other sound, then that sound too may shift to avoid the encroachment, setting off a chain reaction.

Grimm's Law offers an example of a chain shift in which when the voiceless stops (*p*, *t*, *k*) changed to fricatives (*f*, *θ*, *h*) a gap was left that was filled by the next phase of Grimm's Law, voiced stops (*b*, *d*, *g*) > voiceless stops (*p*, *t*, *k*). This in turn left a gap filled by the last phase of Grimm's Law: voiced aspirates (*bh*, *dh*, *gh*) > plain voiced stops (*b*, *d*, *g*). The **Great Vowel Shift** offers another example. See also **maximal differentiation**.

chance similarity (accident)   One of several possible explanations of similarities encountered across languages. A major problem with a number of the proposed **distant genetic relationships** is that often supporters have not demonstrated that the evidence presented could not be accounted for by chance. Conventional wisdom holds that five per cent to six per cent of the vocabulary of any two languages may be accidentally similar; some say four per cent, others seven per cent. Well-known examples of accidental similarities include French *feu* 'fire' and German *Feuer* 'fire'; English *much* and Spanish *mucho* 'much' (Spanish *mucho* < Latin *multus* < **Indo-Europan** **ml̥-to-* 'strong, great'), and English *much* < Old English *micel*, *mycel* 'great', 'much' (< Germanic **mik-ila* < **Proto-Indo-European** **meg-* 'great'); English *day* and Spanish *día* 'day'; Mbabaram (Australia) *dog* 'dog' and English *dog*; Farsi *bad* and English *bad*, Malay *mata* 'eye' and modern Greek *mati* 'eye', Rumanian *fiu* 'son' (< Latin *filius* 'son') and Hungarian *fiú* 'son, boy' (< Proto-Finno-Ugric **poji* 'boy').

change   see **language change**

change and variation   see **variation**

change from above Change from above the speakers' level of awareness. '*Changes from above* are introduced by the dominant social class, often with full awareness. Normally, they represent borrowings from other speech communities that have higher **prestige**, in the view of the dominant class' (Labov 1994: 78).

change from below   Change below the speakers' conscious awareness. '*Changes from below* are systematic changes that appear first in the vernacular, and represent the operation of internal, linguistic factors. At the outset, and through most of their development, they are completely below the level of social awareness' (Labov 1994: 78).

change in progress   Linguistic change that a language is currently in the process of undergoing. The investigation of change in progress is a major focus of sociolinguistics and one of its most significant contributions to historical linguistics. Variation in language, the subject matter of sociolinguistics, often reflects on-going language change, though some **variables** can be stable over time, exhibiting no inclination to move to completion (such as the English stable alternation of -*ing* with less formal '-*in*'). Many variables, however, reveal stages in changes in progress that in time will come to completion, utimately driving one of the variant forms from the language. Investigation of change in progress often involves **apparent-time** studies, some also **real-time** studies.

Chibchan   A **language family** of northern South America and lower Central America, with around twenty languages.

Chimakuan   A small **language family** of two **languages** in western Washington state, Chemakum and Quileute.

Chinookan   A family of languages spoken from Willapa Bay in Washington to Tillamook Bay in Oregon and along the Columbia River and some of its tributaries. The Chinookan homeland was probably around the confluence of the Willamette River and the Columbia River.

chronology   With respect to linguistics, the order in which language changes occur, or the arrangement of these changes according to this order. There are two types of linguistic chronology, **absolute** and **relative chronology**.

clade (from Greek *clados* 'branch')   A term taken from biology where it refers to a group of organisms, for example, a species, that are considered to share a common ancestor, used sometimes in linguistics to refer to a **language family**, a genetic **classification of languages**, usually associated with a **family tree**. See also **genetic model, genetic unit, language classification, taxon**.

cladistic   A term from biology that means pertaining to **clades**, pertaining to the branching sequence in evolution, based on common evolutionary descent, common ancestry; relating to phylogeny, the evolutionary history of a group of organisms. In linguistics sometimes used as roughly equivalent to **genetic classification**. See also **family tree, genetic model, language classification**.

classification, classification of languages (also called

language classification)   Although languages can be classified typologically, geographically and in other ways, normally the term '**classification of languages**' (or '**language classification**') is used to refer to classification of languages according to genetic relationships among related languages.

cline   A term from **dialect geography** that represents an incremental gradience geographically in a particular structural feature; for example, Ibero-Romance word-initial consonant clusters composed of a stop with /l/ such as *pl, *kl; from east to west in the northernmost regions of medieval Spain, Catalan preserved conservative /pl, kl/; in some Aragonese dialects, just to the west, they became /plʸ, klʸ/; in Castilian Spanish, in the center, both merge to /ll/ [lʸ], as they do in west-of-center Asturo-Leonese /č~š/ and in westernmost Gallego-Portuguese /š/: *klave 'key' > Cat. klau [kláw], Arag. klʸau [klʸáw], Cast. llave [lʸáße], Gallego-Port. chave [šávə].

clipping (also called **compression, shortening** and **ellipsis**)   The process of lexical innovation that coins new items by shortening a longer word, eliding material from them – for example, *lab < laboratory, gym < gymnasium, piano < pianoforte, auto < automobile.*

Coahuiltecan   A hypothesis of **distant genetic relationship** that proposed to group some languages of south Texas and northern Mexico: Coahuilteco, Comecrudo and Cotoname, and sometimes also Tonkawa, Karankawa, Atakapa and Maratino (with Aranama and Solano assumed to be varieties of Coahuilteco). Sapir (1929) proposed a broader classification of **Hokan–Coahuiltecan**, joining the Coahuiltecan proposal with the broader **Hokan** hypothesis, and placed this in his even larger **Hokan–Siouan** super-stock. None of these proposals has proven sufficiently robust to be accepted generally. (Sapir 1920, 1929, Campbell 1997: 297–304.)

Cochimí–Yuman A family of languages from Arizona, California and Baja California, with two branches, extinct Cochimí (of Baja California) and the Yuman subfamily (members of which are Kiliwa, Diegueño, Cocopa, Mojave, Maricopa, Paipai and Walapai–Havasupai–Yavapai, among others). Cochimí–Yuman is often associated with the controversial **Hokan** hypothesis, though evidence is insufficient to embrace the proposed relationship.

code A cover term, purposefully vague, used in order to be able to refer to any identifiable, internally consistent means of communication, whether a dialect, sociolect, separate language, sign language, Morse code, drummed language, whistle, speech etc. See also **lect, variety**.

code switching (also sometimes called **code-mixing**). Event or process in which bilingual (or bidialectal) speakers shift between one language (or dialect) and another in the same conversation or discourse, in situations where the interlocutors in conversation have more than one language in common.

cognate A word (or morpheme) that is related to a word (morpheme) in sister languages by reason of these words (morphemes) having been inherited by the related languages from a common word (morpheme) of the **proto-language** from which they descend. For example, Italian *cane* /kane/, Portuguese *cão* /kãũ/, French *chien* /šyẽ/ 'dog', are all cognates, since they descend in these

Romance languages from the same original word in Latin (ancestor of the Romance languages): *canis* 'dog'.

cognate set   A set of cognate words (morphemes), a set of words related to one another in the sister languages because they are inherited and descend from a single word (morpheme) of the **proto-language**.

coinage   Creation of a new word. See also **neologism**.

common   see **proto-language**

comparative linguistics   The subfield of linguistics that compares languages; usually understood as meaning the application of the comparative method to the comparison of languages. Sometimes the term comparative linguistics is used as a synonym or near synonym of **historical linguistics**. See also **comparative method**.

comparative method   The most important method of historical linguistics; a method (or set of procedures) for comparing languages to determine whether they are related and, if related, how they have developed from a common ancestor. The method compares forms from related languages, **cognates**, that have descended from a common ancestral language (the **proto-language**), in order to **reconstruct** the form in that ancestral language and to determine the changes related languages have undergone. It is also the basis for **subgrouping** related languages and establishing their **family tree**. See also **basic assumptions of the comparative method, limitations on the comparative method, reconstruction**.

compensation   see **explanation of linguistic change**

compensatory lengthening   Change in which some sound is lost and simultaneously another segment, usually a vowel, is lengthened, as the name implies, to compensate for the loss – for example, proto-Germanic **tonθ* > Old English *tōθ* 'tooth'; proto-Germanic **fimf* > Old English *fīf* 'five'; proto-Germanic **gans* > Old English *gōs* 'goose'.

conditioned change   A change that takes place only in certain contexts, that is, change that is dependent upon neighboring sounds, upon the changing sound's position within words, or on other aspects of the grammar. Conditioned changes affect only some of a sound's occurrences, those in particular contexts, but not other occurrences that happen to be found in environments outside the restricted situation in which the change takes effect. For example, the Spanish change of Romance *p* to Spanish *b* intervocalically, as in *lupus* > *lobo* 'wolf', is conditioned; only those *p*s that were between vowels became *b*, while *p*s in other positions (for example, at the beginning of words) did not change. A well-known example is the *ruki* rule in Sanskrit; *ruki* is an acronym that stands for the sounds after which /s/ becomes retroflex [ṣ]: s > ṣ after r, u, k, i, y. See also **unconditioned sound change**, *ruki*-**rule**.

conditioned merger   see **merger**

conditioned sound change   see **conditioned change**

Congo-Saharan (Kongo-Saharan) (sometimes called **Niger-Saharan**)   A proposal of a very remote relationship that would lump together **Niger-Congo (Niger-Kordofanian)** and **Nilo-Saharan**, two of Greenberg's (1963) proposed but unconfirmed large African language phyla. The limited evidence cited for this proposal is mostly lexical and morphological look-alikes, which do not eliminate other possible explanations (borrowing, chance etc.), and the presence of typological similarities such as ATR [advanced tongue root] vowel harmony and labiovelars are possibly diffused **areally**.

constraints on the comparative method   see **limitations on the comparative method**

constraints problem   To do with the general constraints on change that determine possible and impossible changes and directions of change. For example, among the constraints on change, Weinreich et al. (1968: 100) postulated that 'no language will assume a form in violation of such formal principles as are ... universal in human languages'. The constraints problem is a central issue in linguistic change; it takes the form of a search for the kinds of linguistic change what will *not* take place. The *irreversibility of mergers* is an example of such a constraint. See also **explanation of linguistic change, Weinreich–Labov–Herzog model**.

contamination   see **blending**

convergence   see **areal linguistics, mixed languages, language contact**

convergence area   see **areal linguistics**

conversion   In **lexicalization**, a change of a grammatical word to a lexical word, for instance *up* as a preposition to *up* as a verb, as in *to up the ante*. Cases of conversion are controversial, since they are counterexamples to the claim of **unidirectionality** (that changes can only go from lexical > grammatical, never the reverse) in **grammaticalization**. See **lexicalization**.

core vocabulary   see **basic vocabulary**

correspondence   see **sound correspondence, correspondence set, comparative method**

correspondence set   see **sound correspondence**

covert prestige   The apparent positive evaluation given to non-standard, low-status, or 'incorrect' forms of speech by many speakers; a hidden or unacknowledged prestige for non-standard **variables** that leads speakers to continue using them, and sometimes causes such forms to spread to other speakers in some cases. The use of variables with covert prestige often functions to identify in-group membership: users who belong to the local community. See also **overt prestige, prestige**.

creole   The traditional definition of a creole is a language descended from a **pidgin** that has become the native language of a group of people – a creole is a pidgin that has acquired native speakers, often when individuals who have only the pidgin language in common marry and their children grow up with the pidgin as their primary means of communication. In this view, the creole differs from the pidgin from which it originated in having a relatively stable though growing grammar with a lexicon, a phonology and an emergent morphology. Many creoles have been noted to have several structural attributes in common, regardless of the languages lying behind the pidgins from which they arose. Some scholars attempt to explain this by claiming that these creoles are the closest languages to an assumed innate universal grammar or bio-program underlying all human language

(Bickerton 1985). Others have sought the explanation in the common European language roots, Portuguese, Dutch, French and English underlying most pidgins and creoles. Unlike languages with standard transmission histories, creoles are sometimes claimed to have no genetic classification – they are assumed not to arise as other languages do – or are claimed to have multiple ancestors, often based on a European language with further input from the native languages of the indigenous population in contact with Europeans that gave rise to the underlying pidgins. Another, more recent, view, however, is that creoles have each a single ancestor: the language of the founder population (usually the dominant European language) that predominates in the development and content of the creole language. This means creoles can be classified genetically, just as other languages, and need not be seen as mixed or having multiple ancestors. Haitian Creole is, in this view, a Romance language closely connected with French, Jamaican Creole a Germanic language closely related to English and so on. See also **pidginization**.

creolization   The process by which a pidgin becomes a creole as it is acquired as a native language by successive generations of children. See also **creole**, *creole continuum*, **decreolization**, **pidgin**.

Cushitic   A family of languages in east Africa. Somali is a major representative of the family. Cushitic is usually classified as a branch of the **Afroasiatic macro-family**.

[D]

Dahl's Law   A sound change that took place in a number of East African Bantu languages; commonly stated as involving the **dissimilation** of aspiration, where the first of aspirated stops in adjacent syllables loses its aspiration and becomes voiced, as in Nyamwezi: -k^hat^hi 'in the middle' > gat^hi, -p^hit^h- 'to pass' > -bit^ha (Mutaka 2000: 253).

daughter language A **language** descended from another language; for example, the various related **sister languages** in a **language family** are each individually daughter languages of the **proto-language**, as, for example, French, Italian, Spanish and several others are daughters of Proto-Romance, and English, German, Swedish and several others are the daughters of Proto-Germanic. See also **comparative method, subgrouping**.

dead language (also called **extinct language**) A language once spoken that no longer has any native speakers. Usually this implies that all its speakers are dead or have abandoned the language and shifted to another; however, a dead language can also be one that did not cease to be spoken directly, but rather changed so much over time that its later descendants are no longer recognized as the same language, as in the case of Latin, of which the various Romance languages are later continuations though Latin itself is a dead language.

deaffrication The process by which an **affricate** loses its stop onset or its fricative-release thereby becoming a unitary sound, just a stop or a fricative. For example, in Yuman languages, the Proto-Yuman affix *$č$ is reflected in Diegueño, Cocopa and Kiliwa by a t. Conversely, in northern Mexican Spanish dialects, $č$ becomes $š$ (also in varieties of Spanish in Andalucia and Panama); for example, *muchacha* 'girl' [mučáča] > [mušáša]. See also **affrication**.

decreolization   A process that applies to a creole under the routine influence of the prestige language from which it derives, so that features of phonology, morphology, syntax and lexicon typical of the creole are progressively supplanted by those of the prestige language. The process may yield what is referred to as a *post-creole continuum*, in which the various degrees to which the creole has accommodated the structures of the prestige language co-exist as *linguistic registers* (variants) available to creole speakers, who may control a range of the variation depending on the interlocutors and social settings. The terms *acrolect* and *basilect* respectively define the uppermost (or highest) and lowest (or deepest) extremes of the continuum. See also **creole**.

degemination   The process by which a **geminate** (a sequence or two identical, adjacent consonants) is simplified when one of the identical consonants is lost resulting in a single unitary sound. For example, Latin geminates were reduced to single segments in Portuguese, as in *gutta* > *gota* 'drop', *caballu-* > *cavalo* 'horse', *annu-* > *ano* 'year', *commodus* 'fitting' > *comodo* 'comfortable', *dissigno* 'I arrange' > *disenho* 'I design'.

degeneration (also called **pejoration**)   Semantic change in which the sense of a word takes on a less positive evaluation in the minds of the language users; an increased negative value judgment. For example, English *silly* 'foolish, stupid' comes from Middle English *sely* 'happy, innocent, pitiable' (from Old English *-sælig* 'blessed, blissful').

degrammaticalization   Change in which a grammatical element becomes more lexical, less grammatical, in content. Used in discussions of **grammaticalization**

to designate violations of **unidirectionality**. See also **lexicalization**.

delabialization   **Sound change** in which a consonant loses **labialization**, that is, loses lip-rounding as a secondary manner of articulation, as, for example, in Nootka, where $k^w > k$ word-finally or in Kiliwa (Yuman, Baja California) in which $k^w > k$ before another labial segment, vowel or consonant (Mixco 2000a, 2000b). The opposite of delabialization is **labialization**.

deletion (also sometimes called *elision*)   A change in which a sound is lost – removed from a language – often in a conditioned change with loss in only certain environments. See also **loss**.

Dené-Caucasian, Dené-Sino-Caucasian   A proposed distant genetic relationship, associated initially with a number of Russian scholars, that would link *Burushaski*, *North Caucasian*, **Basque** and **Sino-Tibetan**, the so-called 'Na-Dené' languages, and for some also **Yenisseian** (Bengston 1991, 1992, 1997, Blažek and Bengston 1995, Shevoroshkin 1991). However, since not even -Na-Dené has been satisfactorily demonstrated, Na-Dené could hardly be shown successfully to be connected to these various Old World groups. The proposed **macro-family** has also been called the *Macro-Caucasian phylum* and *Sino-Caucasian*. See **Na-Dené**.

de Saussure, Ferdinand   see **laryngeal theory, diachronic linguistics**

descent group   Johanna Nichols' term for any group of genetically related languages, 'the basic building block of linguistic populations' (Nichols 1997: 360), which includes **families** and **stocks**. See also **language family, genetic unit**.

desemanticization   see **semantic bleaching**

devoicing   **Sound change** in which a sound becomes voiceless, that is, is converted into a voiceless sound. For example, devoicing of final stops in some languages (German, Russian) and of final sonorants in others (several languages of Mesoamerica) is quite common. See also **voicing**.

diachronic   Having to do with the temporal dimension, change over time, from Greek *dia-* 'through' + *chronos* 'time'. See also **diachronic linguistics, synchrony**.

diachronic linguistics   Roughly equivalent to **historical linguistics**, having to do with the study of language in its temporal dimension, through time. See also **diachronic, diachrony, synchrony**.

diachrony   Temporal dimension, viewed through time. With respect to language, the historical investigation of linguistic elements, of language changes and evolution. The concept is often associated with **de Saussure's** distinction between **diachronic** and **synchronic linguistics**. See also **diachronic linguisticstics**.

dialect   Any regional or social **variety** of a single language that is mutually intelligible with other dialects of the same language and that differs in some definable features from other varieties of that language. Linguists with UK associations distinguish **accents** – varieties that differ from one another primarily only in pronunciation. In the

USA 'accent' is not used in this sense, rather these varieties, too, are called dialects. Since the entities called 'accents' are rarely distinguished by pronunciations alone, but also typically correlate with regional differences in vocabulary and sometimes aspects of grammar, the distinction between 'accent' and 'dialect' may not be a particularly useful one.

The term 'dialect' does not refer to little-known or minority languages (sometimes called 'exotic' languages), though it has sometimes been used, particularly in the past, in this sense. Dialect is also sometimes used to refer to a **daughter language** of a **language family**.

See **cline, dialect continuum, new-dialect formation, dialect geography, variety**.

dialect atlas (also called **linguistic atlas**)   An atlas (collection of maps) of a geographical region that shows the distribution of particular linguistic forms, especially traits that vary in the dialects of the region. See also **dialect geography**.

dialect borrowing (also called **dialect mixture**)   The diffusion of linguistic traits from one dialect to another, influence of one dialect on another. Sometimes invoked in the past to explain what otherwise might appear to be instances of exceptions to the **Neogrammarian** regularity of **sound change**. See also **lexical diffusion, wave theory**.

dialect continuum (also called **dialect chain**)   A group of geographically contiguous dialects in which the dialect traits that separate those that are in direct contact are fewer but increase in number and complexity with an increase in distance. Thus, in a dialect continuum, neighboring dialects are mutually intelligible to a high degree, whereas ease of comprehension decreases as one approaches the most distant extremes of the chain or continuum. For example, it was said that in medieval times a traveler from Paris to Rome, progressing through that part of the Romance dialect continuum, would never experience anything but the gradual adjustments needed in communicating from stop to stop. However, speakers from the extremes encountering each other abruptly might experience considerable difficulty in communicating due to greater differences. See also **cline, dialect geography, mutual intelligibility**.

dialect formation   see **new-dialect formation**

dialect geography   The study of regional **dialects**, particularly to explain their distribution, usually presented in dialect maps. Along with historical linguistics, dialect geography was one of the earliest fields to arise in the scientific study of language in nineteenth-century Europe. Among its originators and earliest practitioners were Georg Wenker (Germany) and Jules Gilliéron (France). They created the field that studies regional language variation, typically determining the nature and degree of the geographical limits of speech **varieties** within a common language. These studies typically result in **dialect maps** and **dialect atlases** that focus on any number of diagnostic features defining the regional varieties, cumulatively revealing the distribution and frequency of dialect variation for a given language. Dialectologists were often believed to be the intellectual foils of the **Neogrammarians**, providing seeming evidence to counter their claim of exceptionless **sound change**. The slogan of some dialectologists was 'every word has its own history', challenging the claim of regularity of **sound change**. See also **cline, dialect atlas, new-**

dialect continuum, dialect formation, dialect, variable, variation.

dialect mixing   see **dialect borrowing**

dialectology   see **dialect, new-dialect formation, dialect geography**

diffusion   The spread of linguistic traits (words, sounds, grammatical material etc.) from one language or dialect to another. 'Diffusion' is often used as a near synonym of **borrowing**.

When diffusion of structural features across the languages of a particular region takes place, we speak of a **linguistic area**. See also **areal linguistics, language contact, lexical diffusion**.

diglossia   The situation in which a speech community has two or more varieties of the same language used by speakers under different conditions, characterized by certain traits (attributes) usually with one variety considered 'higher' and another variety 'lower'. Well-known examples are the high and low variants in Arabic, Modern Greek, Swiss German and Haitian Creole. Arabic diglossia is very old, stemming from the difference in the classical literary of the language of the Qur'an, on one side, and the modern colloquial varieties, on the other side. These languages just named have a superposed, high variety and a vernacular, lower variety, and each languages has names for their high and low varieties, which are specialized in their functions and mostly occur in mutually exclusive situations. To learn the languages properly, one must know when it is appropriate to use the high and when the low variety forms.

Typically, the attitude is that the high variety is the proper, true form of the language, and the low variety is wrong or does not even exist. Often the feeling that the high variety is superior derives from its use within a religion, since often the high language is represented in a body of sacred texts or esteemed literature. Diglossia is associated with the American linguist Charles A. Ferguson. Sometimes, following Joshua Fishman, diglossia is extended to situations not of high and low variants of the same language, but to multilingual situations in which different languages are used in different domains, for example, English is regarded as 'high' in areas of India and of Africa and local languages as 'low' or vernacular. This usage for diglossia in multilingual situations is resisted by some scholars.

diphthongization   Change in which a single vowel turns into a diphthong; that is, a pure vowel changes so that it takes on an additional vowel quality within a syllable or, a single, simple vowel changes into a sequence of two or more vocalic articulatory gestures that together occupy the nucleus of a single syllable. For example, in the Great Vowel Shift, English original long high vowels /i:/ and /u:/ diphthongized to /ai/ and /au/ respectively, as in /mi:s/ > /mais/ 'mice' and /mu:s/ > /maus/ 'mouse'. See also **breaking**; see **monophthongization**.

directionality of change   The typical or expected direction of a linguistic change. Some kinds of changes, found repeatedly in independent languages, typically go in one direction (A > B) but usually do not (sometimes never) go in the other direction (B > A). For example, numerous languages have changed s > h, but change in the other direction, h > s, is almost unknown. Cases such as this illustrate the 'directionality' of the change. There is a known directionality to many grammatical changes, as well. For example, the change of Postposition > Case affix is frequent, but a change of Case affix > Postposition is extremely rare.

Known directionality of change helps in linguistic **reconstruction**. If, for example, in two sister languages, s of Language$_1$ correspondences to h in Language$_2$, $*s$ is reconstructed for the parent sound in the **proto-language**, and the change is postulated that $*s > h$ in Language$_2$. The alternative with $*h$ for the original sound and a **sound change** of $*h > s$ in Language$_1$ is unlikely, since it goes against the known direction of change. Similarly, if in two sister languages a postposition 'with' in Language$_1$ correspondences to a commitative case affix (also meaning 'with') in Language$_2$, then the postposition is reconstructed for the proto-language, with the change of postpostion 'with' > commitative case in Language$_2$, since the known directionality of this change makes the alternative (with a reconstructed commitative case and a postulated change of commitative case > postposition 'with') highly improbable.

dispersal of languages   see **language dispersal**

displacement   A kind of **synecdoche** (also called **ellipsis**) in which one word absorbs part or all of the meaning of another word with which it is linked in a phrase (usually Adjective–Noun, typically with loss of the absorbed or 'displaced' part), for example, *capital* from *capital city*, where the notion of 'city' has been absorbed into the word 'capital'. *Contact(s)* < *contact lens(es)* and *private* 'ordinary, regular soldier' < *private soldier* are other examples.

dissimilation (sometimes also called **dissimilatory change**) Change in which a sound becomes less similar to another sound. Dissimilation (increased difference between sounds) is the opposite of **assimilation** (increased similarity among sounds). For example, Latin *arbore* 'tree' changed to *árbol* in Spanish, where the change *r > l* in this word made the two *r*'s less similar to one another (*r ... r > r ... l*). Similarly, Latin *libellum* 'level' changed to *nivel* in Spanish, in which sequence of two *l*'s was made less similar by changing one to *n* (*l ... l > n ... l*). In some English dialects the sequence of two nasals is dissimilated in *chimney* to become *chimley* (or *chimbley*). **Grassmann's Law** is a famous case of dissimilation.

distant genetic relationship A genetic relationship between languages that are only remotely related. Many distant genetic relationships have been postulated among languages not known to be related, where, owing either to the lack of convincing evidence or to doubts about the methods used (or both), the hypotheses are disputed. Some examples of these controversial proposals of distant genetic relationship are Altaic, Amerind, Eurasiatic, Nostratic, Proto-World, and many others (see Campbell 2003, Campbell and Poser in press). Also spoken of in terms of **macro-family, remote relationship,** *long-range hypothesis of relationship*. See also **multilateral comparison**.

divergence Process by which languages or dialects (sometimes, sounds, constructions etc.) become more different from one another. See also **diversification**.

diversification (sometimes also called **divergence**) The process by which languages split up into related languages and then typically become increasingly more distinct from one another. All languages (and varieties of language) change, and regional **dialects** can arise through these changes. As further changes accumulate, these dialects can develop into distinct languages; that is, they diversify, become divergent. The related languages of **language families** all descend from an original **proto-language** that diversified over time. Thus, English is, essentially, a much-changed 'dialect' of Proto-Germanic, that has undergone successive linguistic changes to make it a different language from German, Swedish and its other sisters. Each proto-language was once a single language, which diversified, resulting in its **daughter languages**. As a proto-language (for example, **Proto-Indo-European**) diversifies, it develops daughter languages (such as Proto-Germanic, Proto-Celtic etc.); a daughter (for instance Proto-Germanic) can subsequently itself diversify and develop daughter languages of its own (such as English, German etc.), then the descendants (English, German etc.) of that daughter language (Proto-Germanic) could continue diversifying, so that, for example, modern English dialects in the future, if they undergo enough change, could become distinct languages making English then their proto-language.

donor, donor language   The language from which something is borrowed by another language; the language that contributes linguistic traits to another in the process of **borrowing**. See also **borrowing, language contact, recipient language**.

drag chain   see **pull chain**; see **chain shift**

Dravidian   The **language family** that embraces most of the languages of South Indian, as well as a few others elsewhere on the Indian subcontinent – some twenty-five languages spoken by about 200 million speakers.

drift   Development in which related languages (or varieties of languages) come to share some similarities due to parallel innovations after diversifying from a common source. Sapir (1921: 150) introduced 'drift' by saying that 'language moves down time in a current of its own making. It has a drift'. Of examples of drift, he wrote:

> The momentum of ... drift is often such that languages long disconnected will pass through the same or strikingly similar phases ... The English type of plural represented by *foot: feet, mouse: mice* is strictly parallel to the German *Fuss: Füsse, Maus: Mäuse* ... Documentary evidence shows conclusively that there could have been no plurals of this type in Primitive Germanic ... There was evidently some general tendency or group of tendencies in early Germanic, long before English and German had developed as such, that eventually drove both of these dialects along closely parallel paths. (Sapir 1921: 172.)

Sapir's lack of elaboration left room for interpretations. In some interpretations of what Sapir meant by 'drift', the related languages share some linguistic characteristics because they are believed to have inherited a shared tendency or propensity to development in a similar fashion after separation, though what linguistic facts might explain such inherited shared tendencies are left unspecified. In other interpretations, drift seems almost mystical, and in any case imprecise and abstract. More modern interpretations hold that drift is just expected change, given the typical **direction-**

ality of many changes and the structural properties **sister languages** share through inheritance from their parent language. Scholars following these interpretations find that, given the same set of starting circumstances (shared inherited structural properties) and the frequent directionality of change in particular typological contexts, there is nothing mystical about the parallel but independent changes that related languages may undergo; rather, in many cases, given the shared attributes related languages start out with and the directionality of many changes, these changes are not at all unexpected.

E

ease of articulation (as a cause of sound change)   The idea that certain sound changes (or other changes that, among other things, also involve the phonetic shape of forms) take place to make this part of the language easier to pronounce. A tendency towards ease of pronunciation has often been thought a major factor in the **explanation of linguistic change**. Often there are natural explanations lying behind changes said to be for ease of articulation. For example, the frequent change of voicing of intervocalic stops seen in many languages facilitates pronunciation, but lying behind that are apparently the workings of the human speech organs – it is just easier to allow the vocal cords to continue vibrating for the vowels (voiced) and for the stop between them than to have to vibrate for one vowel, stop the vibration of the vocal cords for the stop, and then start up the vibration again for the following vowel. See also **simplification**.

economy   A concept akin to the philosophical and scientific principle embodied in Okham's Razor, which states that a hypothesis that employs fewer entities and simpler logic is superior to one that does not. The criterion of economy in **reconstruction** holds that when multiple alternatives are available the one that requires the least number of reconstructed elements with the fewest independent changes is most likely to be correct. For example, in **phonological reconstruction** economy is achieved in a proto-system with smaller numbers of phonemes, involving the fewest changes to account for the **reflexes** found in the **cognates** of **daughter languages**. See also **ease of articulation, simplicity**.

e-grade   see **ablaut**

elaboration   Johanna Nichols' term for language **diversification**, the splitting of a language into distinct **daughter languages**. Nichols (1990) asserts that characteristically at the initial split up of a language, the number of branches will tend to be two (two to three prior to extinction of some of the branches, and 1.6 afterward).

Elamite-Dravidian, Elamo-Dravidian (also called Dravidian-Elamite)   A controversial hypothesis of **distant genetic relationship** between Elamite and Dravidian. David McAlpin (1974, 1981) presented a reasonable though not thoroughly convincing case for a genetic relationship between Dravidian and Elamite (an ancient, long-extinct isolate of the Persian Gulf).

elevation (also called **amelioration**)   Semantic changes in which the meaning of a word shifts towards a more positive value in the minds of the language's users; an increased positive value judgment, as in *pretty*, which in its Old English form meant 'crafty, sly'. Also called **amelioration**.

ellipsis   see **clipping**

embedding problem   Concerns the question, how is a given language change embedded in the surrounding system of linguistic and social relations? How does the greater environment in which the change takes place influence the change? That is, the parts of a language are tightly interwoven, often in complex interlocking relationships, so that a change in one part of the grammar may impact on (or be constrained by) other parts of the grammar. Also, language change takes place in a social environment, where differences in a language may be given positive or negative sociolinguistic status, and this sociolinguistic environment plays an important role in change. See also **Weinreich–Labov–Herzog model**, **explanation of linguistic change**.

emphatic foreignization   Change in the pronunciation of a word to make it seem more foreign-sounding. Cases of emphatic foreignization usually involve slang or high registers, and often place names, as in the pronunciations of *Azerbaijan*, *Beijing* and *Taj Mahal* with the somewhat more foreign-sounding 'zh' [ž], [azerbaižan], [beižɪŋ], [taž mahal] rather than the less exotic but more traditional pronunciations with 'j' [ǰ], [azerbaijan], [beijɪŋ], [taǰ mahal]. In English, *coup de grâce* (literally, 'blow/hit of grace', borrowed from French) is often pronounced without the final *s*, as /ku də gra/, rather than as /ku də gras/ because many English speakers expect French words spelled with an *s* to lack it in the pronunciation; on this basis they have eliminated the sound even though it is pronounced in French. See also **hypercorrection**.

endangered language   Language (also **dialect**) in danger of no longer being spoken, of being lost and becoming extinct. Endangered languages are often spoken by communities with some disadvantage relative to other languages (or dialects) in their vicinity. Those with a relatively lower socioeconomic status or less political influence often become endangered. Dialects or languages enjoying a higher position in such a hierarchy, spoken by segments of the same community or constituting contiguous communities, tend to displace the smaller, less valued or less influential languages. This process has been referred to as **language shift** and usually manifests itself, in the advanced stages, when the children of the disadvantaged linguistic community cease to acquire their **heritage language** (or dialect) as their first language in the home or community, opting for one with greater prestige or power. Effort to sustain or revive the viability of endangered languages is called **language revitalization**, the goal of which is **reversal of language shift** (Fishman 1991; Hinton and Hale 2001). Language endangerment is considered the most serious problem confronting contemporary linguistics. See also **language death, obsolescence.**

English Great Vowel Shift   see **Great Vowel Shift**

epenthesis   The **insertion** of a sound into a word (from Greek *epi* 'in addition' + *en* 'in' + *thesis* 'placing'). **Prothesis, anaptyxis, excrescence** and **paragoge** are kinds of epenthesis. Epenthesis can be a **synchronic** or a **diachronic** process. See also **insertion.**

erosion (sometimes also called **phonetic attrition**) Progressive reduction or **loss** of linguistic material, especially the phonetic form of words (or morphemes) by **sound change**. Sometimes also called (**phonetic**) **attrition**.

Eskimo-Aleut   A **language family** of some seven or so **languages** with many **varieties** extending from Siberia across North America to Greenland. The Aleut branch, of the Aleutian islands, has two main **dialects**. The Eskimo subfamily has Yupik (Yup'ik), a branch with five languages, and the Inuit-Inupiaq branch of related dialects extending from Alaska across Canada to Greenland.

Eskimo–Uralic   A proposed remote relationship between the **Eskimo–Aleut** and **Uralic** families, not widely supported by scholars. (Campbell 1997: 284.)

esoteric language   see **esoterogeny**

esoterogeny   'A sociolinguistic development in which speakers of a language add linguistic innovations that increase the complexity of their language in order to highlight their distinctiveness from neighboring groups' (Foley 2000: 359); 'esoterogeny arises through a group's desire for exclusiveness' (Ross 1996: 184). Through purposeful changes, a particular community **language** becomes the 'in-group' code which serves to exclude outsiders (Thurston 1989: 556–7, Ross 1997: 232). A difficulty with this interpretation is that it is not clear how the hypothesized motive for these changes – conscious (sometimes subconscious) exclusion of outsiders (Ross 1997: 239) – could be tested or how changes motivated for this purpose might be distinguished from changes that just happen, with no such motive. The opposite of esoterogeny is **exoterogeny**.

Ethiopian linguistic area   A **linguistic area** that includes: **Cushitic** (Beja, Awngi, Afar, Sidamo, Somali etc.), Ethiopian **Semitic** (Ge'ez, Tigre, Tigrinya, Amharic etc.), **Omotic** (Wellamo [Wolaytta], Kefa, Janjero [Yemsa] etc.), Anyuak, Gumuz and others. Among the traits they share are: (1) SOV (Subject-Object-Verb) basic word order, including postpositions; (2) subordinate clause preceding main clause; (3) gerund (non-finite verb in subordinate clauses, often inflected for person and gender); (4) a 'quoting' construction (a direct quotation followed by some form of 'to say'); (5) compound verbs (consisting of a noun-like 'preverb' and a semantically empty auxiliary verb); (6) negative copula; (7) plurals of nouns not used after numbers; (8) gender distinction in second and third person pronouns; (9) reduplicated intensives; (10) different present tense marker for main and subordinate clauses; (11) the form equivalent to the feminine singular used for plural concord (feminine singular adjective, verb or pronoun used to agree with a plural noun); (12) a singulative construction (the simplest noun may be a collective or plural and it requires an affix to make a singular); (13) shared phonological traits such as *f* but no *p*, palatalization, glottalized consonants, gemination, presence of pharyngeal fricatives. (Ferguson 1976; Thomason 2001; compare Tosco 2000.) See also **areal linguistics**.

Etruscan   Long extinct **isolate** of northern Italy attested in many short funerary inscriptions, found on funerary urns, in tombs and on sarchophagi. Etruscan was considered a **language** of culture by the ancient Romans and its alphabet became the model for the alphabets of various languages of the region and of western Europe.

etymology   Broadly, the study of the origin or history of words (from Greek *etumon* 'true' [neuter form], that is, 'true or original meaning of a word'). In another sense, the origin and history of a specific word. The earlier sense of etymology, in classical antiquity, was the unfolding of the true meaning of words, but this shifted to the modern sense of the search for word histories and the origin of words.

etymological dictionary   A dictionary that presents what is known (and in some instances also what is hypothesized or even speculated) about the origin and history of words (and other linguistic material) in a particular **language** or **language family**. Some notable examples of etymological dictionaries are Bloch and von Wartburg (1968) for French, Corominas and Pascual (1980) for Spanish, Kluge 1975 for German, and Pokorny (1959/ 1969) for **Indo-European**.

etymological doublet   see **learned loan**

etymon   An earlier linguistic form (usually a word) from which a later form or forms (typically a word or words) is/are derived. For example, since English *foot* derives from **Proto-Indo-European** **ped-*, the Proto-Indo-European word is the etymon of the English word. In another looser sense, an etymon is just an entry in an **etymological dictionary**.

euphemism   A word (or phrase) that replaces another that is considered obscene, offensive, taboo or that otherwise causes discomfort. An example is the euphemistic replacement of words for 'toilet' by *lavatory, bathroom, restroom, washroom* and numerous other words. Also, sometimes the process by which such replacements take place. See also **taboo avoidance**.

Eurasiatic Greenberg's (2000, 2002) hypothesis of a **distant genetic relationship** that would group **Indo-European, Uralic–Yukaghir, Altaic, Korean–Japanese–Ainu, Nivkh, Chukotian** and **Eskimo–Aleut** as members of a very large 'linguistic **stock**'. While there is considerable overlap in the putative members of Eurasiatic and **Nostratic** there are also significant differences. Eurasiatic has been sharply criticized and is largely rejected by specialists (Georg and Vovin 2003, 2005).

evaluation problem Concerns the questions of how speakers of a language (members of a speech community) evaluate a given change, what the effect is of their evaluation on the change and what the effects are of the change on the language's overall structure. See **Weinreich–Labov–Herzog model, explanation of linguistic change.**

'every word has its own history' – *'chaque mot a son histoire'* The slogan, usually associated with **dialectologists** who opposed the **Neogrammarian's** notion of the **regularity** (exceptionlessness) of **sound change,** is often attributed to Jules Gilliéron, author of the *Atlas linguistique de la France* (1902–1910), the dialect atlas of France (see Gilliéron 1921, Gilliéron and Roques 1912). It is also credited to Hugo Schuchardt (1868), though, a contemporary of the Neogrammarians, of whose claims he was critical. The idea behind the slogan is that a word's history may be the result of various influences and changes, both internal and external to the language or dialect in question, and these may be quite different from those involved in another word's history, so that each word has its own (potentially quite different) history.

exception A form that has failed to undergo expected

changes or to conform to expected patterns or processes of the language in question. A fundamental premise of the **Neogrammarians** was that 'sound laws suffer no exceptions'. In many instances, subsequent examination proved that that an underlying regularity could be found, and such seeming exceptions were explained as being due to **borrowing, analogy** or **dialect mixture**. More recently, advocates of **lexical diffusion** have claimed that some sound changes progress through the lexicon at different rates, thus possibly yielding exceptions due to incomplete spread of a rule throughout the lexicon. This view is challenged by some and qualified by others.

excrescence (from Latin *ex* 'out' + *crēscentia* 'growth', 'outgrowth')   A **sound change** in which a consonant emerges (grows) between two consonants, or, put differently, in which a consonant is inserted between consonants. Excrescence is often thought to be motivated by greater ease of pronunciation in the transition between consonants within consonant clusters. An example in English is the inserted *b* of *thimble*, from earlier *thimle*. In Spanish, *tendré* 'I shall have' comes from *tenré* (originally from **tener-é*). See **epenthesis**.

exoteric language   see **exoterogeny**

exoterogeny   'Reduces phonological and morphological irregularity or complexity, and makes the language more regular, more understandable and more learnable' (Ross 1997: 239). 'If a community has extensive ties with other communities and their ... language is also spoken as a contact language by members of those communities, then they will probably value their language for its use across community boundaries ... it will be an "exoteric" lect [variety]' (Ross 1997: 238). Use by a wider range of speakers makes an exoteric **lect** subject to considerable variability, so that innovations leading to greater simplicity will be preferred.

The claim that the use across communities will lead to **simplification** of such languages does not appear to hold in numerous known cases (for example, Arabic, Cuzco Quechua, Georgian, Mongolian, Pama-Nyungan, Shoshone etc.). The opposite of exoterogeny is **esoterogeny**.

explanation of linguistic change   Rendering understandable why languages change; statement of the reasons why languages change as they do. Important to the explanation of linguistic change is the identification of *causal factors*, both those that always bring about change and those that create circumstances known to facilitate change but in which, even when the factors are present, the change does not always take place.

It is usual to distinguish internal and external causal factors. **Internal causal factors** rely on the limitations and resources of human speech production and perception, physical explanations of change stemming from the physiology of human speech organs and cognitive explanations involving the perception, processing or learning of language. These internal factors are largely responsible for the natural, regular, universal aspects of language and language change; they can compete in their interactions in ways that make prediction of language change difficult. **External causal factors** lie outside the structure of language itself and outside the human organism; they include such things as expressive uses of language, positive and negative social evaluations (prestige, stigma), the effects of literacy, prescriptive grammar, educational policies, political decree, language planning, **language contact** and so on. Many see the crux of explanation of linguistic change as being tied up with the tension or competition in the two poles of language, between the communicative needs of the speaker (language production) and those of the hearer (language perception, parsing). A change affecting one of these can have consequences for the other that either precipitate subsequent changes or impede changes that would be favored in the other pole of language.

The recognition of a large number of interacting and competing causal factors in language change means that at present we are unable to predict linguistic change fully. Some scholars who equate 'explain' with 'predict' conclude from this that it is impossible to explain linguistic change. The need to postulate competing principles and multiple causes renders law-like explanations of the sort sought in physics and chemistry impossible in **historical linguistics**. Some believe that the current unpredictability may ultimately be overcome through research to identify causal factors and to understand the complex ways in which these factors interact and hope for a greater predictive ability in the future. Many others, though, hold that not only will absolute predictability probably never be possible, but that neither is it necessary for explanation – in just the same way that evolution by natural selection explains many changes in biology though it does not 'predict' fully the evolutionary changes that it explains. Change within complex systems (languages, living organisms, societies) involves many factors that are interrelated in complex ways – and more than one cause is frequently involved in particular changes, making prediction difficult. Given that multiple causes frequently operate simultaneously in complex ways to bring about particular linguistic changes, to explain linguistic change it is necessary to investigate the multiple causes and how they jointly operate in some cases and compete in others to determine the outcome of linguistic change.

See also **ease of articulation, teleology of language change, Weinreich–Labov–Herzog model.**

expressive symbolism   see **sound symbolism**

extension   A **mechanism of syntactic change** that results in changes in surface manifestation but does not involve immediate modification of the underlying structure, usually found following or in association with **reanalysis.** For example, after the reanalysis of *be going to* created a new future auxiliary from what earlier had been only a verb of motion with purposive complements, by extension the change was later extended so that the new future could occur with complement verbs the use of which was not possible in the former sense of a simple verb of motion (as in *It is going to rain, Charles is going to like Camilla* and *Hillary is going to go to Congress*). See also **analogy, mechanisms of change.**

external causal factors, external factors   Factors that help to explain language changes that lie outside the structure of language itself and outside the human organism. They include such things as expressive uses of language, positive and negative social evaluations (prestige, stigma), the effects of literacy, prescriptive grammar, educational policies, political decree, language planning, **language contact** and so on. See **internal causal factors; borrowing, language contact.**

external evidence   Non-linguistic evidence about the history or prehistory of a **language** or set of languages – for example, facts from archaeology, ethnohistory, human genetics and other sources of non-linguistic information – that have bearing on language history.

extinct language   A **language** that has ceased to have any native speakers either because all the speakers are dead or because they abandoned this language completely in a shift to another language. See **dead language**. See also **obsolescence**.

Eyak–Athabaskan   A large North American **language family** of some forty member **languages** spread from Alaska to Mexico that contains Eyak of Alaska and the Athabaskan subfamily. See also **Athabaskan**.

$\boxed{\text{F}}$

fading   see **semantic bleaching**

family   see **language family**

family tree (also sometimes called by the German equivalent **Stammbaum**)   The set of genealogical relationships holding among the **languages** of a **language family**, and, also, the graphic representation of the genealogical classification of the languages of a language family. Is also used in English. See also **genetic relationship, classification of languages, subgrouping, family-tree model**.

family-tree model   The standard means for representing the **genetic relationships** among **languages**, shown in terms of a genealogical tree. In the three diagram or model, the branching – represented by the lines between individual languages and the nodes or **subgroups** to which they belong – shows which languages that are more closely related to one another within each of the branches and what their intermediate parent language within the **language family** is. These branches are called the **subgroups** of the language family. The family-tree model can represent directly only the relationship of inheritance from a common ancestor, of descent with change, but has no way of representing directly other kinds of relationships that might hold among the languages, for example relationships among the languages having to do with borrowing, language contact, or geographical location – for this, historical linguistics has other methods and techniques.

Also sometimes **genetic model, cladistic** model; sometimes the German equivalent, *Stammbaumtheorie*, is used in English.

farming/language dispersal model   An approach to explaining the dispersals and spreads of many **language families**, from Colin Renfrew and Peter Bellwood, which emphasizes agriculture as the primary agent of **language** dispersal. Renfrew (1996: 70), for example, argues: 'farming dispersals, generally through the expansion of populations of farmers by a process of colonization or demic diffusion, are responsible for the distribution and areal extent of many of the world's language families'. Linguists have criticized the model for being too single-minded, leaving out of the equation the many other factors known to be involved in the dispersal of various languages and language families.

Finno-Ugric   Well-known **language family** – actually a large branch of the larger Uralic family – which extends from the Baltic Sea to northern Siberia. Finno-Ugric **languages** include Finnish, Estonian, Hungarian and some twenty-five others.

First Germanic Consonant Shift   see **Grimm's Law**

flapping (also sometimes called **tapping**)   **Sound change** (or phonological rule) that converts /t/ and /d/ to a flap (tap) in certain contexts, especially associated with American English. Also sometimes called **tapping**.

focal area   see **dialect geography, relic area**

folk etymology (also called **popular etymology**)   A kind of *analogical change* in which speakers assign meaning associations to forms (words or morphemes) that the forms did not originally have based on their resemblance to other forms in the language, and on the basis of these new meaning associations either the original form is changed or new forms based on the new meaning associations are created. That is, speakers believe the word or morpheme to have an etymology or analysis that is false from the perspective of the form's earlier history. An example is the English word *hamburger*, whose true etymology is from German *Hamburg + -er*, 'someone from the city of Hamburg'; hamburgers are not made of 'ham', but speakers associated *hamburger* with *ham* and on this basis created new words such as *cheeseburger*, *fishburger* etc. Another example comes from the Spanish *vagabundo* 'vagabond, tramp', which gave rise in some varieties of Spanish to *vagamundo* 'tramp, vagabond', through the folk-etymological association with *vaga* 'wander, roam, loaf' and with *mundo* 'world'. See also **analogy**.

foreignization   see **emphatic foreignization**

fortition   see **strengthening**

fossilization   Process by which a form or construction ceases to be used freely, becomes frozen, unproductive. See **unproductive**.

founder effect   see **founder principle**

founder principle (also called **founder effect**)   A claim that structural peculiarities of a given **dialect** or **language** have their roots in the variety of language spoken by the population (or populations) that originally introduced the language to the region. This principle is seen to limit the influence of the language spoken by new groups entering an established community by asserting that the original group determines the patterns to be followed, even when newcomers may be very numerous. Founder effect involves long-term persistent influences, where the language of the founders persists in spite of onslaught from later varieties (Mufwene 2001).

frequency (as a factor in language change)   Higher frequency of usage appears to contribute to the preservation of certain **language** traits, in particular of irregular features, by resisting the pressure for regularization (**analogical leveling**). Examples of this phenomenon are the persistence in **Indo-European** languages of the suppletive Indo-European personal pronouns and the suppletive forms of the verb *to be*. For example, the irregularities seen in English *be, is, are, was, were* are thought to have persisted due to the high frequency of their occurrence.

fricativization   A sound change (also a synchronic phonological process) in which some sound becomes a fricative (spirant). For example, it is not unusual for an affricate to be weakened to a fricative or for stops to become fricatives between vowels or before obstruents.

functional load (also called **functional yield**)   Pertains to the number of forms a particular linguistic element serves, especially the number of words/morphemes exhibiting a particular phonemic contrast. It is often assumed that phonemes with a low functional load – those that distinguish words in only a few minimal pairs – may be more subject to **loss** or **merger** than phonemes with a high functional load – those that distinguish many minimal pairs – since the loss of contrast with low functional yield would not result in as many formerly distinct words/morphemes becoming homophonous as the loss of a distinction involving phonemes of higher functional yield that distinguish many words from one another. The concept is also sometimes applied to grammatical morphemes, in which case it is usually the morphemes that occur frequently or in many constructions that are considered to be higher in functional load.

functional yield   see **functional load**

fusional, fusional language   In **language typology**, the type of **language** in which the boundary between morphemes within words is often not clear, where, for example, a morpheme can simultaneously encode more than one meaning, as in English *feet*, simultaneously 'foot' and 'plural'. See also **descent group, inflectional**.

G

Gê, Gêan (also called **Jê, Jêan**)   A family of some twelve **languages** spoken mostly in Brazil. Usually assumed to be a branch of the hypothesized but unconfirmed **Macro-Gê**.

gemination (from Latin *gemināti̇̄on-em* 'doubling', related to *geminus* 'twin') **Sound change** that involves the doubling of consonants, either by a single consonant geminating (doubling), or by two distinct consonants changing into a sequence of two identical adjacent consonants. An example of the first form is seen in Finnish dialects, in which in a sequence of short vowel – short consonant – long vowel (VCVV) the consonant is regularly geminated, as in *osaa* > *ossaa* 'he/she knows', *pakoon* > *pakkoon* 'into flight (fleeing)'. Examples of the second kind are seen in the changes in Italian, as in *nokte* > *notte* 'night', *somno* > *sonno* 'sleep'.

genetic affiliation   see **genetic relationship**

genetic classification   see **classification**

genetic linguistics   see **comparative linguistics**

genetic model   see **family-tree model**

genetic relationship (also **genetic affiliation**)   The relationship between **languages** that have a common ancestor; languages that are members of the same **language family**. See also **comparative linguistics**, **comparative method**, **language family**.

genetic unit   Term more or less equivalent to **language family** if **isolates** are considered language families (families with but a single **daughter language**, a single member); that is, a term of convenience that makes it possible to group **language family** and **isolate** together under a single name. See also **descent group, language family.**

Germanic   A subfamily (**subgroup**) of **Indo-European**, the branch to which Dutch, English, German, Icelandic, Norwegian, Swedish and Gothic belong, among others.

Gilyak   see **Nivkh**

global etymologies   see **Proto-World**

gloss   Generally, a short translation of a word, phrase or sentence in one language to give its meaning equivalence in another language, for example German *Hund* 'dog' – where 'dog' is the gloss for the German word *Hund*. Also, an interlinear or marginal notation (typically in an ancient manuscript) giving the translation or explanation of a word or brief passage. Also an entry in a glossary, as for example this entry *gloss* in this glossary of historical linguistics.

glottalic theory   The hypothesis that the sounds traditionally reconstructed for **Proto-Indo-European** as voiced stops, **b, *d, (*g^j), *g, *g^w*, should instead be reconstructed as ejectives (glottalized), **p', *t', (*k^{j'}), *k', *k^{w'}*). The hypothesis is especially associated with Gamkrelidze and Ivanov (1973) and Hopper (1973), though there are also other supporters with other versions. It is argued that the glottalic reinterpretation of Proto-Indo-European stops makes for a typologically more plausible consonant system. It was claimed that the traditional reconstruction with three stop series – plain voiceless (**p, *t, (*k^j), *k, *k^w*), voiced stops (**b, *d, (*g^j), *g, *g^w*), voiced aspirate series (**bh, *dh, (*g^jh), *gh, *g^wh*) – was typologically unusual, since voiced aspirates rarely occur in languages that do not also have voiceless aspirated stops. Therefore, Gamkrelidze and Ivanov proposed that the plain voiceless series represented aspirated consonants (*ph, *th, (*kʲh), *kh, *kʷh). The traditional *b is very rare, perhaps fully missing, in Proto-Indo-European words; this would be typologically unusual for a language with the three stop series as traditionally reconstructed; however, it is not unusual cross-linguistically for the labial to be missing from the series of glottalized consonants. Similarly, **Indo-European** roots did not contain two voiced stops (for example, no *ged or *deb sequences) – it would be typologically unusual for a language to have a constraint on two voiced stops in the same root, but cases were observed of languages with a constraint against the occurrence of two glottalized consonants in the same root.

Nevertheless, any gains the revised glottalic reconstruction may seem to achieve in terms of the typological plausibility of the reconstructed system appear to be offset by the numerous typologically implausible sound changes that would be needed to derive various of the modern languages from the reconstructed sounds of the glottalic theory. The glottalic theory reconstructions remain controversial, not accepted by the majority of Indo-Europeanists.

glottochronology (also often held to be equivalent to lexico-statics)   A proposed method for calculating the dates of linguistic diversification – when splits among sister languages within a language family occurred – originally formulated by Morris Swadesh. It is based on the controversial premise that there exists a constant **rate of loss** of lexical items over time in **basic** (or **core**) **vocabulary**. The items are drawn from *Swadesh's lists* of 100 and 200 words of basic vocabulary that are assumed to have little or no cultural content and, thus, presumably to be relatively resistant to borrowing through cultural contact. These lists involve concepts for which equivalents can be expected in (nearly) all languages, for example, words for certain natural phenomena, body parts, kinship terms, low numbers, basic pronouns, primary colors etc. Swadesh believed the rate of retention of basic vocabulary was constant over time – eighty-six per cent for the 100-word list – and the same for all languages. It was believed that the number of years since their separation could be calculated, based on the assumption of a constant rate of retention and given the proportion of retained lexical cognates between compared languages. Glottochronology is presumed to reflect the degree of relatedness and the relative distance between languages in a **family tree**. It has also been used in an additional way. Some practitioners base their assumptions of genetic relatedness more or less exclusively on its calculations, often without the benefit of the **comparative method**.

All the basic assumptions of glottochronology have been challenged, and it is rejected by most linguists. (Embleton 1986; Gudschinsky 1956.) See also **basic vocabulary, lexicostatistics, Swadesh list**.

glottogonic Pertaining to the first emergence of human language, also to the period of time when human language was thought to have first developed, as well as to nineteenth-century linguistics dedicated to the study of the origin and earliest development of human language. Glottogonic interpretation saw modern languages as mere decayed versions of the more 'perfect' classical languages. Many believed in two separated stages of language development, in the first of which language began with simple roots (often monosyllabic) and, through **agglutination**, developed morphological and grammatical properties in its progress towards perfection. In the later stage, through **sound change** and **analogy**, languages began to decay. Glottogonic views linked early notions of language typology and language evolution ('progress'), both usually associated with assumptions that language and reason ('mind') evolved together.

The glottogonic view was perhaps the principal difference between the **Neogrammarians** and their predecessors. The Neogrammarians rejected the assumed growth process (which they called 'glottogonic speculation') and the separation of stages of language development (change towards perfection versus language decay); they declared the processes of change (sound change, analogy) were the same from the **proto-language** onward, and that there was no need to assume independent lexical roots lying behind grammatical endings and certainly no separation of stages of 'progress' versus 'decay'. The glottogonic view was dismissed. See also **glottogony**.

glottogony The emergence (origin) of human language, the study of the origin and earliest development of human language, the name for a kind of linguistics concerned with the origin and evolution of language. Glottogony was a frequent term in the nineteenth century, now very rarely seen. See also **glottogonic**.

grade   see **ablaut**

grammatical alternation   see **Verner's Law**

grammatical change   A term that can refer to either

morphological or **syntactic change**. In another sense, the English equivalent of German *grammatischer Wechsel* (**grammatical alternation**), which has to do with differences in related forms in morphological paradigms produced by some sound changes, associated especially with **Verner's Law**. In generative linguistics, grammatical change is sometimes equivalent to any structural change in a language. See also **morphological change, syntactic change; Verner's Law**.

grammatical conditioning   see **morphological conditioning**

grammatical reconstruction   see **syntactic reconstruction**

grammaticalization   Change that attributes 'a grammatical character to a formerly independent word' (Meillet 1912: 132); 'grammaticalization consists in the increase of the range of a morpheme advancing from a lexical to a grammatical or from a less grammatical to a more grammatical status' (Kurłowicz (1965: 52).

Grammaticalization is typically associated with **semantic bleaching** and *phonetic reduction*, and thus Heine and Reh (1984: 15) define grammaticalization as 'an evolution whereby linguistic units lose in semantic complexity, pragmatic significance, syntactic freedom, and phonetic substance'.

A frequently cited example of grammaticalization is English *will*, which originally meant 'want', as its German cognate, *will* '(he/she) wants', still does. English *will* became semantically bleached (lost its sense of 'want') and was grammaticalized as a 'future' marker. *Will* also undergoes **phonetic erosion**, as in contractions such as *I'll, she'll, my dog'll do it*.

grammaticization   see **grammaticalization**

grammatischer Wechsel   see **Verner's Law**

Grassmann's Law   A well-known **sound change** of **Indo-European** found by Hermann Grassmann that involves regular **dissimilation** in Greek and Sanskrit where in roots with two aspirated stops the first dissimilates to an unaspirated stop. The consonants involved are voiced aspirated stops in Sanskrit and voiceless aspirated stops in Greek:

> Sanskrit *bhabhūva* > *babhūva* 'became' (reduplication of root *bhu-*)
> Greek *phéphūka* > *péphūka* 'converted' (reduplication of *phú-* 'to engender').

A well-known Greek example is: *trikh-ós* 'hair' (genitive singular) / *thrík-s* (nominative singular), where *trikhos* comes from **thrikh-os*, to which Grassmann's law has applied dissimilating the *th* because of the following aspirated *kh* (**th ... kh > t ... kh*); in *thríks* 'hair', from **thrikh-s*, the *kh* lost its aspiration because of the following *s* (**khs >ks*), and so Grassmann's law did not apply to this form, there no longer being two aspirated stops.

Great Vowel Shift (also called the **English Great Vowel Shift**) A **chain shift** (series of **sound changes**) in Middle English (with its main effects of the fifteenth and early sixteenth centuries) in which low and mid-long vowels were raised:

> /æ:/ > /e:/ (and later > /i:/) (as in *beak*)
> /a:/ > /e:/ (as in *make*)
> /e:/ > /i:/ (as in *feet*) and /o:/ > /u:/ (as in *boot*),

and the long high vowels were diphthongized:

/iː/ > /ai/ (as in *mice*)
/uː/ > /au/ (as in *mouse*). See also **chain shift.**

Grimm's Law   A set of interrelated **sound changes** associated with Jakob Grimm (of Grimm brothers fairytale fame) involving changes in the stop series from **Proto-Indo-European** to Proto-Germanic:

1. voiceless stops > fricatives: p, t, k > f, θ, h, respectively
2. voiced stops > voiceless stops: b, d, g > p, t, k, respectively
3. voiced aspirated stops > plain voiced stops: *bh*, *dh*, *gh* > *b*, *d*, *g*, respectively

This means that words in Germanic languages, because they inherit the results of these changes from Proto-Germanic, show the effects of these changes, while cognate words from other **Indo-European** languages (not from the Germanic branch) do not undergo the changes, as seen in the following examples, in which the French cognates have not undergone Grimm's Law, but the English forms have:

French	*English*
*p > f in Germanic:	
pied	foot
père	father
*t > θ in Germanic:	
trois	three
tu	thou
*k > h in Germanic:	
cœur	heart
cent (< kent-)	hundred
*d > t in Germanic:	
dent	tooth
deux	two

 *g > k in Germanic:
grain   corn
genou   knee
 *bh > b in Germanic:
frère (< *bhrat-)   brother
etc.

Gulf   Hypothesis of a **distant genetic relationship** proposed
by Mary R. Haas (1951, 1952, 1960) that would group
Muskogean, Natchez, Tunica, Atakapa and **Chitimacha,**
no longer supported by most linguists (see Campbell
1997: 306–9).

 H

Hamito-Semitic   see **Afroasiatic**

haplology (from Greek *haplo-* 'simple, single')   **Sound
change** in which a repeated sequence of sounds is simplified to a single occurrence. For example, some English
speakers reduce *library* to *'libry'* [láibri] and *probably* to
'probly' [prábli]; English *humbly* comes from *humblely*
by haplology.

heritage language (or **dialect**)   see **endangered language**

heteroclitic noun class   A class of nouns rare or fossilized in
the **Indo-European** languages except in **Hittite** and some
of the other older Indo-European languages, characterized by an alternation of /n/ with /l/ or /r/: Sanskrit
údhar (nominative), *údh-n-as* (accusative) 'udder',
Latin *iecur* (nominative), *iec-in-oris* ('dative') 'liver',
Proto-Indo-European **iék^w-r* (nominative), **i(e)k^w-én-s*
(genitive)   'liver';   Proto-Indo-European   **péHur,*

p(e)H-uén-s 'fire', Hittite *pahhur, pahh-uen-as* 'fire' (Trask 2000: 148).

High German Consonant Shift see **Second Germanic Consonant Shift**

historical linguist   A linguist who studies **language change**.

historical linguistics (sometimes called **historical and comparative linguistics**)   The study of **language change**, of how and why languages change. See also **diachronic linguistics, philology**.

historical syntax   The study of syntactic change.

Hittite   One of several extinct languages in the Anatolian branch of **Indo-European**; the subfamily also includes Lydian, Palaic, Luvian, Lycian and Carian. Hittite is best known from the library of cuneiform tablets from 1600–1200 BC found at Boğaz Köy, in modern Turkey. The Anatolian languages reflect a degree of archaism with respect to **Proto-Indo-European**, retaining a **heteroclitic noun class** (rare or fossilized except in Hittite) and *laryngeal consonants* (mostly changed to vocalic elements in other Indo-European languages). See also **heteroclitic noun class, laryngeal hypothesis**.

Hmong-Mien see **Miao-Yao**

Hokan   A controversial hypothesis of **distant genetic relationship** proposed by Dixon and Kroeber (1913a, 1913b, 1919) among certain languages of California; the original list included *Shastan, Chimariko,* **Pomoan**, *Karok* and *Yana*, to which they soon added *Esselen*, **Yuman** and later *Chumashan, Salinan, Seri* and

Tequistlatecan. Later scholars, especially Edward Sapir, proposed various additions to Hokan. Many 'Hokan' specialists doubt the validity of the hypothesis (Mixco 1997).

Hokan-Coahuiltecan   A hypothesis of **distant genetic relationship** proposed by Edward Sapir (1929) that would join **Hokan** and **Coahuiltecan**, two proposals of remote linguistic relationships that are doubted by most specialists. See also **Hokan, Coahuiltecan.**

Hokan-Siouan   Sapir's (1929) proposed superphylum which would group **Hokan-Coahuiltecan**, Siouan and several other families and isolates; mostly abandoned today. (Campbell 1997: 260–305.) See also **Hokan, Coahuiltecan, Siouan, Hokan-Coahuiltecan.**

homeland   see **linguistic homeland**

homophony   see **avoidance of homophony**

Hurrian   Name of the language of the Hurrians, a people who entered northern Mesopotamia around 2300 BC and vanished by around 1000 BC. It is believed that the Hurrians came out of Armenia and spread over parts of southeast Anatolia and northern Mesopotamia. The *Urartian* language is thought to be descended from Hurrian. Hurrian texts, written in cuneiform script, have been found in the ancient archives of Urkesh and from the Hittite archives of Hattusas, modern Boğaz Köy. Hurrian domination in the area was replaced by **Hittite.**

hyperbole (from Greek *hyperbolē* 'excess') **Semantic change** in which meaning shifts because of exaggeration by overstatement. For example, English *terribly,* *horribly*, *awfully* and similar words today mean little more than 'very', a way of intensifying the meaning of whatever adjective they may modify; by overstatement they came to have no real connection with their origins, *terror, horror, awe* etc.

hypercorrection A kind of **analogical change** in which speakers make an attempt to change a form from a less prestigious variety to make it conform with how it would be pronounced in a more prestigious variety but in the process overshoot the target so that the result is erroneous from the point of view of the prestige variety being mimicked. For example, *for you and I* (for Standard English *for you and me*) is a hypercorrection based on stigmatized use of *me* as subject pronoun in instances such as *Billy and me saw a rat* or *me and him chased the rat*. Speakers, in attempting to correct instances such as these sometimes go too far and hyper-correct instances of *me* to *I* even when *me* is an object (direct or indirect) and correct in Standard English (as in *Jimmy gave the rat to Billy and me* (hypercorrected to ... *to Billy and I*). Some Spanish dialects change *dr* to *gr*, as in *magre* 'mother' (Standard Spanish *madre*), *pagre* 'father' (< *padre*), *piegra* 'stone' (< *piedra*), *Pegro* 'Pedro' (< *Pedro*); speakers of these dialects often attempt to change these *gr* pronunciations back to *dr* to match the prestigious *dr* of Standard Spanish, but in doing this, they sometimes hypercorrect by changing some instances of *gr* to *dr* which in fact are *gr* in the prestige variety, as for example *suedros* 'parents-in-law' (Standard Spanish *suegros*), *sadrado* 'sacred' (< *sagrado*).

hyperforeignization see **emphatic foreignization**

I

iconicity   A non-arbitrary, motivated link between a linguistic form's phonetic shape and its meaning. In historical linguistics, it is often assumed that iconic material may resist changes that would lessen the iconic link between form and meaning, and, also, that change can be favored to increase iconicity. For example, English *peep* should have undergone the **Great Vowel Shift** to give /paip/ (as *pipe* actually did, from earlier /pi:p/), but such a change would have decreased the connection between the sound of 'peep' and the noise birds make, and therefore the change was resisted.

Functionalist linguists explain the structure of language on the basis of **function**; for them, *function drives shape* – a very iconic notion. For them, the way grammatical constructions are packaged reflects their function, their role in communication. The functional explanations offered often involve assumptions about perception and production, about what would facilitate the hearer's being able to process (parse) what he/she hears and about what would aid the speaker to produce (package) the intended message. Iconicity plays an important role; it has to do with claims that the structure of language somehow reflects the structure of the world. For example, we say in English (and equivalently in almost all languages) 'Hillary entered the room and she sat down on the couch', where the order of the clauses reflects the temporal sequence in the real-world events, with Hillary first entering and then subsequently sitting. The fact that the linguistic order reflects the order of events as they transpired in the real world reflects the *linear order iconic principle*: The order of clauses in coherent discourse will tend to correspond to the temporal order of the occurrence of the depicted events

(Givón 1990: 971). Iconic motivations have been proposed for many pieces of grammar and for correspondences among pieces of grammar (see Haiman 1985, Givón 1990). Iconic principles that have been proposed include:

Quantity (or economy)
1. A larger chunk of information will be given a larger chunk of code.
2. Less predictable information will be given more coding material.
3. More important information will be given more coding material.

Proximity
4. Entities that are closer together functionally, conceptually, or cognitively will be placed closer together at the code level, i.e. temporally or spatially.
5. Functional operators will be placed closest, temporally or spatially at the code level, to the conceptual unit to which they are most relevant (Givón 1990: 969–70).

The term 'iconicity' owes its origin to Peirce's theory of signs, in which icons are one kind of sign, though its usage in linguistics is now independent of its origins. See **onomatopoeia, sound symbolism**.

ideophone, ideophonic   see **sound symbolism**

idiolect   The **language** ('**dialect**') of a single particular speaker; a variety of a language unique to an individual seen in the grammatical and lexical choices, characteristic pronunciation or idioms that characterize that individual's speech. See also **lect**.

idiomaticization   see **lexicalization**

independent parallel innovation   see **parallel innovation**

indeterminacy of reconstruction   see **limitations of the comparative method, reality of reconstructions**

Indian linguistic area   see **South Asian linguistic area**

Indic   see **Indo-Aryan**

Indo-Aryan (also called **Indic**)   Branch of **Indo-European**, closely related to the **Iranian** languages within the larger **Indo-Iranian** subgroup, located in the Indian subcontinent and contiguous regions. The Indo-Aryan (Indic) languages include Bengali, Gujerati, Hindi-Urdu, Panjabi, Sindhi. Nepali, Romani (the language of the Rom or Gypsies) and many others.

Indo-European   The best known of all **language families**. Branches of the Indo-European family include *Anatolian*, *Indo-Iranian*, **Tocharian**, Hellenic (Greek), Armenian, **Italic**, *Celtic*, **Germanic**, *Balto-Slavic* and *Albanian*, among others. By extension, Indo-European is an adjective referring to the cultures, religions and peoples associated with these languages. See also **Proto-Indo-European**.

Indo-Germanic   see **Indo-European**

Indo-Hittite hypothesis   The hypothesis, associated with Edgar Sturtevant, that **Hittite** (or better said, the **Anatolian** languages, of which Hittite is the best known member) was the earliest Indo-European language to split off from the others. That is, this hypothesis would have Anatolian and Indo-European as sisters, two branches of a Proto-Indo-Hittite. The more accepted view is that Anatolian is just one subgroup of Indo-European, albeit perhaps the first to have branched off, hence not 'Indo-Hittite' but just 'Indo-European' with Anatolian as one of its branches. In fact the two views differ very little in substance, since, in either case, Anatolian ends up being a subfamily distinct from the other branches and in the view of many the first to branch off the family.

Indo-Pacific   A rejected proposal of **distant genetic relationship** in which Joseph H. Greenberg (1971: 807) argued that 'the bulk of the non-Austronesian languages of Oceania from the Andaman Islands on the west of the Bay of Bengal to Tasmania in the southeast [excluding Australia] forms a single group of genetically related languages'. The hypothesis is mainly concerned with the non-Austronesian **'Papuan'** languages of New Guinea, but also includes several groups outside New Guinea. The major groups involved are: (1) Andaman Islands, (2) Timor-Alor, (3) Halmahera, (4) New Britain, (5) Bougainville, (6) Central Melanesia, (7) Northern New Guinea, (8) Tasmania, (9) Western New Guinea, (10) Northern New Guinea, (11) South West New Guinea, (12) Southern New Guinea, (13) Central New Guinea, (14) North East New Guinea, (15) and (16) Eastern New Guinea. As van Driem (2001: 139–40) pointed out, Greenberg's 'Indo-Pacific' hypothesis is essentially identical to Finck's (1909) family, which he called the 'Sprachen der ozeanischen Neger' [languages of the Oceanic Negroes] based on racial notions; the name 'Indo-Pacific' had already been used for this group, rooted in the 'Pan-Negrito theory', the 'crinkly hair hypothesis' (van Driem 2001: 140). The Indo-Pacific hypothesis is rejected by nearly all scholars today.

Indo-Uralic   The hypothesis that the **Indo-European** and **Uralic language families** are genetically related to one another. While there is some suggestive evidence for the hypothesis, it has not yet been possible to confirm the proposed relationship.

inflectional, inflectional language   In language typology, the type of language that undergoes inflection (or inflexion), the modification or marking of a word so that it reflects grammatical information, such as grammatical gender, tense, person, number etc. Inflectional type contrasts with **agglutinative** and **isolating**-type languages. See also **fusional**.

inkhorn term (also **inkhornism, inkpot term**)   Referring to an obscure and ostentatious word, usually derived from Latin or Greek, used more in writing than in speech (hence the name); a word deliberately borrowed or created in the sixteenth and seventeenth centuries, based primarily on Latin but also on Greek, with borrowings also from French, Italian and elsewhere, sometimes just for pedantry, sometimes intended to enrich the language, to fill supposed gaps in English vocabulary. There was considerable difference of opinion over the value of inkhornisms at the time. Though most did not survive, many were accepted and became a regular part of English vocabulary, for example *anachronism, allure, atmosphere, autograph, jurisprudence, appropriate, conspicuous, adapt, alienate, benefit, disregard, emancipate, eradicate, excavate, harass* and hundreds of others.

innovation   Loosely, any change a language undergoes.
   James Milroy (1992) gives 'innovation' a more technical sense. Milroy's conception of linguistic change is linked with his stand on the **actuation problem**. He tries 'to approach actuation by first making a distinction between *speaker* and *system*, and within this a distinction between speaker-innovation and linguistic change' (p. 200). He distinguishes *innovators* ('marginal' persons with weak ties to more than one group who form a bridge between groups) from *early adopters* (those who are 'relatively central to the group') (p. 184); the former are associated with 'innovations' that become 'change' [in his technical sense] only when taken up by early adopters, from whom the innovation/change 'diffuses to the group as a whole' (p. 184). See also **speaker-innovation**.

insertion   Any one of a number of changes that insert some linguistic material or element that was not previously present, usually said of sound changes that produce sounds not formerly found where the insertion takes place, as in **anaptyxis, epenthesis, excrescence, paragoge, prothesis** etc.

interference   In **language contact** (and second language acquisition), the carry over of traits from one's native (or dominant) **language** to another language that one speaks. See also **phonetic interference, transfer**.

internal causal factors, internal factors   Factors that rely on the limitations and resources of human speech production and perception to help to explain **language change**; physical explanations of change stemming from the physiology of human speech organs; and cognitive explanations involving the perception, processing or learning of language. These internal factors are largely responsible for the natural, regular, universal aspects of language and language change. The opposite of **internal factors** is **external factors**. See also **explanation of linguistic change, external causal factors**.

internal reconstruction   A method for inferring aspects of the history of a language from the evidence found in that language alone. When a language undergoes changes, traces of the changes are often left in the language's structure as allomorphic variants or irregularities of some sort. Internal reconstruction compares such variants and irregularities – different allomorphs in paradigms, derivations, stylistic variants and the like. It can recover valuable information when applied to: (1) **isolates** (languages without known relatives); (2) alternating forms in reconstructed **proto-languages** to see even further back into the past; and (3) individual languages to arrive at an earlier stage to which the **comparative method** can then be applied to compare such an internally reconstructed older stage of a language with related languages in the family. The result of internal reconstruction is labeled 'pre-', as in, for example, *Pre-English*, to English as internally reconstructed. For instance, for the English alternating forms /lɔŋ/ (as in *long*) – /lɔŋg/ (as in *longer*), /strɔŋ/ (*strong*) – /strɔŋg/ (in *stronger*) etc., we reconstruct the final /g/, *lɔŋg, *lɔŋg-er, *strɔŋg, *strɔŋg-er and postulate a change that final -g is lost after the nasal (*lɔŋg* > *lɔŋ*), retained when non-final (*lɔŋger*). (Actually, we posit *lɔng with *n* > *ŋ* before *g*, with the final *g* later being lost, that is, *lɔng > lɔŋg > lɔŋ).

Internal reconstruction can often recover **conditioned changes**, but cannot recover **unconditioned sound changes** or changes where too much subsequent change has obscured the original conditioning, that is, the environments in which the change took place.

inversion   see **rule inversion**

'invisible hand' theory   Approach to explaining **language change** advocated by Rudi Keller (1994) based on Adam Smith's account in economics. Central to this model is the notion that change in a given direction comes about as though directed by an 'invisible hand' through the separate behavior of many individual speakers whose actions are not intended to produce the particular linguistic change but are, rather, directed to their own other ends. The particular change is an unanticipated by-product of that behavior directed to other purposes. See also **teleology of language change**.

Iranian   A subfamily of **Indo-European**, closely affiliated with **Indo-Aryan** (**Indic**) in the higher-order **Indo-Iranian** branch of **Indo-European**. It includes Avestan, Baluchi, Kurdish, Persian, Pashto etc.

Iroquoian   A **language family** of eastern North America, among the members of which are Cherokee, Tuscarora, Huron, Seneca, Cayuga, Oneida and Mohawk.

isogloss   In **dialectology**, a line on a map that represents the geographical boundary (limit) of regional linguistic variants; by extension, isogloss also refers to the **dialect** feature itself, the actual linguistic phenomenon that the line on a map represents. For example, in the USA the *greasy/greazy* isogloss corresponds roughly to the Mason–Dixon line that separates the North Midlands from South Midlands; it runs across the middle of the country until it dives down across southeastern Kansas, western Oklahoma and Texas. North of the line *greasy* is pronounced with *s*; south of the line it is pronounced with *z*.

isolate (also called **language isolate**, sometimes **isolated language**)   A **language** with no known relatives, that is, a family with but a single member. Some well-known isolates are: Ainu, Basque, Burushaski, Etruscan, Gilyak (Nivkh), Nahali, Sumerian, Tarascan and Zuni. See also **language family**.

isolating language   In typology, the type of **language** in which each morpheme is a separate word, that is, where there is no bound morphology, and grammatical markers are independent words. Chinese is a much-cited example; many of the languages of southeast Asia are also isolating languages. See also **agglutination, synthetic language**.

Italic   A branch of **Indo-European** containing Oscan, Umbrian and Latin-Faliscan, ancient languages of Italy. Latin is the best known of these, and the **Romance** languages descend from Latin.

J

Japanese   see **Japanese-Ryukyuan**

Japanese-Ryukyuan   A small **language family** (sometimes called **Japonic**) made up of Japanese, spoken by the approximately 126 million – mostly in Japan – and Ryukyu, a closely related language of Okinawa (sometimes called 'Okinawan dialect'). A number of hypotheses have attempted to connect Japanese/Japanese-

Ryukuan with other languages in broader genetic groupings, but without success. The most persistent has been
the attempt to link Japanese with the disputed **Altaic**
hypothesis.

Junggrammatiker   see **Neogrammarians**

K

Kartvelian (also called **South Caucasian**)   A **language family**
of the south Caucasus region comprising Georgian,
Megrelian, Laz and Svan.

Keresan, Keres   Spoken in two principal varieties – Eastern
and Western – in seven Indian Pueblos in New Mexico.
Western Keresan includes Acoma and Laguna while
Eastern Keresan consists of Cochiti, Zia–Santa Ana and
San Felipe–Santo Domingo, varieties found in the Rio
Grande Valley between Santa Fe and Albuquerque.

Keresiouan   see **Almosan-Keresiouan**

Khoisan   A proposed **distant genetic relationship** associated
with Greenberg's (1963) classification of African
languages, which holds some thirty non-Bantu click
languages of southern and eastern Africa to be genetically related to one another. Greenberg originally called
his Khoisan grouping 'the Click Languages' but later
changed this to a name based on a created compound of
the Hottentots' name for themselves, Khoi, and their
name for the Bushmen, San. Khoisan is the least accepted
of Greenberg's four African **phyla**. Several scholars agree
in using the term 'Khoisan' not to reflect a **genetic relationship** among the languages but, rather, as a cover term
for all the non-Bantu and non-Cushitic click languages

of eastern and southern Africa, perhaps the result of **areal linguistic** influences.

Kiowa–Tanoan   A **language family** composed of Kiowa (of the Great Plains, now in Oklahoma) and the Tanoan languages, spoken in various pueblos of the Southwest of the USA. The Tiwa branch of Tanoan includes Taos, Picuris, Isleta and Sandia; the Tewa branch has Hopi Tewa (Hano) and Santa Clara–San Juan; and the Towa branch is represented by Jemez (Miller 1959).

koiné   Originally, the variety of **Greek** that became general in the eastern Mediterranean after Alexander the Great's conquests in the fourth century BC. A term in **sociolinguistics** for any variety of language that comes about through the leveling of differences among **dialects**, often cited as a factor in **new-dialect formation** where multiple dialects are involved in the process. See also **koineization**.

koineization   Process by which a **variety** of a **language** comes about through the leveling of differences among multiple **dialects** that enter into the make-up of the new, leveled variety, often cited as a factor in **new-dialect formation** where multiple dialects are involved in the process. See **koiné, swamping**.

Korean   A language **isolate**, spoken by over 70 million in the two Koreas and adjacent areas. Korean is sometimes cited as an example of an **agglutinative** language, and a **language** with SOV (Subject-Object-Verb) word order. Some scholars classify Korean in a single family with Japanese; however, this is a controversial hypothesis. Korean is often said to belong with the **Altaic** hypothesis, often also with Japanese, though this is not widely supported.

Kurgan hypothesis   The hypothesis, proposed and defended by Marija Gimbutas (1963), that the Kurgan archaeological culture from the Pontic and Volga steppes of the Black Sea represented the speakers of **Proto-Indo-European**. The correlation between Proto-Indo-European and Kurgan culture has support, though there is also debate. In Gimbutas' view, the expansion of Kurgan culture corresponds in time and area with the expansion of **Indo-European** languages outward from a homeland in this area, and correlates with the spread to other areas of such typically Indo-European things as horses, wheeled vehicles, double-headed axes, small villages, pastoral economy and patriarchal society.

$\boxed{\text{L}}$

labialization   **Sound change** in which lip-rounding is added as a secondary manner of articulation to a consonant, for example $k > k^w$ after o in Wichí (Matacoan language of Argentina). The opposite of labialization is **delabialization**, in which labialization is lost.

Lallwörter   see **nursery words**

language   The notion 'language', so intuitively clear, has proven remarkably difficult to define at times. At issue are the distinction between separate languages and dialects of a single language and the extent to which political, cultural and other matters enter the definition of particular languages. For linguists, the criterion of **mutual intelligibility** separates distinct languages from mere dialects of the same language: any **varities** that are not mutually intelligible to their respective speakers are clearly separate languages, and any varieties that are totally intelligible to their respective speakers are clearly dialects of the same language. Still, it is not that simple, since some ambiguous cases stem from situations of **non-reciprocal intelligibility**, where speakers of one 'language' understand those of another language, but speakers of that other language do not understand speakers of the first, as is usual with Spanish and Portuguese, where Portuguese speakers often understand Spanish while Spanish speakers typically do not understand Portuguese. Another complication comes from the non-linguistic factors. Weinreich said a language is 'a dialect which has an army and a navy'. This emphasizes the fact that the definition of *language* is not strictly a linguistic matter, but often involves political and cultural considerations. For example, Swedish and Norwegian, though largely mutually intelligible, are considered separate languages for political reasons.

language area   Terrence Kaufman's term for cases in which it is difficult to distinguish between quite different dialects of a single language and closely related languages, where 'there are clear boundaries between ... communities ... yet there is a high degree of mutual intelligibility' (Kaufman 1990: 69). Easily confused with **linguistic area**, the term is not particularly felicitous. See also **dialect**; contrast with **linguistic area, areal linguistics**.

language change   Any mutation, alteration or innovation in language. How and why languages change is the central concern of **historical linguistics**.

language classification   see **classification (of languages)**

language contact The use of more than one language in the same place. More specifically, the influence of one language upon another, and, in the sense most common in **historical linguistics**, any change due to influence from neighboring languages. Language contact describes the circumstances under which multilingual speakers of two or more contiguous languages facilitate the transfer of linguistic traits from one language into another. This process may affect any component of the grammar (that is, phonology, morphology, syntax, semantics, lexicon etc.). The most typical consequence of language contact is **lexical borrowing,** and such introduced vocabulary may serve as the conduit for other influences, ultimately affecting areas of grammar beyond the lexicon, especially sounds. For example, borrowing of French words like *beige* and *rouge* into earlier English not only expanded English vocabulary but also changed English's phonological inventory by adding the phoneme ž. Another example is the introduction of the plural suffix /-s/ into German by way of loanwords from other European languages that have such a plural. Contact can also lead to the rise of a **linguistic area** (see **areal linguistics**) within which languages come to share numerous non-inherited, diffused linguistic traits. **Mixed languages, pidginization** and **creolization** are extreme consequences of language contact. See also **borrowing, creole, naturalization, pidgin, transfer, interference.**

language death (also spoken of in terms of **endangered language,** *linguistic obsolescence, language contraction, language attrition, moribund language, language erosion, language decay, disintegrating language, vestigial language, imperfect language learning, semi-speaker*) Language extinction, the process through which languages cease to be spoken and become extinct.

Typically, language death involves language shift and replacement where the obsolescent language becomes restricted to fewer and fewer individuals who use it in ever fewer contexts, until it ultimately vanishes altogether. Language endangerment is considered by many scholars to be the most serious problem in linguistics today, and many languages have already become extinct, for example, Cornish, Coptic, Dalmatian, Etruscan, Gothic, Hittite, Manx, Old Prussian, Sumerian, and many many more. Different **kinds of language death** that have been talked about are: (1) *Sudden language death* ('linguacide', 'language death by genocide', 'physical' or 'biological' language death): the abrupt disappearance of a language because almost all of its speakers suddenly die or are killed, examples include Tasmanian and Yana. (2) *Radical language death*: rapid language loss due either to severe political repression under which speakers stop speaking the language for self-defense, or, to rapid population collapse due to destruction of culture, epidemics etc. (3) *Bottom-to-top language death*: attrition of the repertoire of stylistic registers from the bottom up ('latinate pattern') with use continuing only in formal genres; loss comes first in contexts of domestic intimacy and the language is confined to use only in elevated contexts. (4) *Gradual language death* (the most common): loss of a language due to gradual shift to the dominant language, with an intermediate stage of bilingualism in which the dominant language comes to be employed by an ever-increasing number of individuals in a growing number of contexts. This typically exhibits a *proficiency continuum* determined principally by the age of the speakers. (5) Aspects of a language that is otherwise almost totally lost may linger to function *emblematically*, as *boundary markers* or *intimate codes*, to signal group identity, solidarity or intimacy or to distinguish outsiders. Things retained that may function emblematically can include greetings, obscenities, toasts, songs, rhymes and jokes, or jargonized languages. (6) So-called *rememberers*, who were never competent speakers, but only learned isolated words and fixed phrases. Their 'remembered' forms rarely contain phonetic material not found in their dominant language.

It is argued that dying languages can change in ways not available to fully viable languages and can also undergo normal kinds of linguistic change. For example, they can undergo overgeneralization of unmarked features, overgeneralization of unusual features, loss or reduction in phonological contrasts, and loss of phonological rules; they tend to develop **variability**, can undergo structural changes due to influence from the dominant language, suffer **morphological** and **syntactic reduction**, exhibit a preference for **analytic** constructions over **synthetic** ones, and suffer **stylistic shrinkage**.

language dispersal The spread of a **language** or of languages geographically. Frequently associated with language **diversification** since the spread of languages to new territory often goes hand in hand with their diversification into families of related languages. There are numerous ideas about what causes languages to diversify involving, for example, migration, war and conquest, trade, geographical isolation, cessation of communication, social and economic organization (e.g. mounted warriors with expansionist proclivities, militaristic patriarchies), linguistically-marked group identity entailing rights to resources, technological advantage (in, for example, food production, herding, navigation, metallurgy, military organization), various religious notions, such as divine vengeance for the construction of the Tower of Babel. The **farming/language dispersal model** advocated by Colin Renfrew and Peter Bellwood is one approach, criticized for not taking into account the range of other factors that can and do contribute to language dispersal and spread.

language family   A group made up of languages that have developed from a common ancestor, genetically related languages. Some well-known language families are **Algonquian, Athabaskan, Austronesian, Bantu, Cushitic, Dravidian, Indo-European, Mayan, Otomanguean, Pama-Nyungan, Salishan, Semitic, Sino-Tibetan, Siouan, Tai, Tupian, Turkic, Uralic** and **Uto-Aztecan**. There are some 300 independent language families (or **genetic units**, which include both families of languages and language **isolates**) in the world.

Language families can be of different magnitudes, so that some larger-scale families may include smaller-scale families among their **subgroups** or branches. The term 'subgroup' (also **subfamily, branch**) refers to a group of languages within a language family that are more closely related to each other than to other languages of that family – a subgroup is a branch of a family. As a **proto-language** (for example, **Proto-Indo-European**) diversifies, it develops **daughter languages** (such as Proto-Germanic, Proto-Celtic); if a daughter (say Proto-Germanic) subsequently splits up itself and develops daughter languages of its own (English, German etc.) they then constitute members of a subgroup (the **Germanic** languages), and the original daughter language (Proto-Germanic) becomes an *intermediate* proto-language, occupying the roles of both parent and descendant. Germanic, while a language family in its own right, is at the same time a *subfamily* (subgroup) of the broader, higher-order Indo-European family of which it is a branch.

Language family names often end in the suffix *–an* (as for example, Indo-European, Dravidian etc.). Some end in *-ic* (as in Cushitic, Turkic, Uralic [called Uralian by some] etc.) Such suffixes are helpful, since some language families are named for a prominent language in the family and without the suffix it would be difficult to distinguish the whole family from that single member language; for example, Mayan is a family of some thirty-one languages, while Maya (or Yucatec Maya) is one of the languages of this family; Tucano is a single language, and Tucanoan is the family to which Tucano belongs.

There are a number of terms for postulated but unproven, more inclusive hypothesized language families, proposed **distant genetic relationships**): **stock**, **phylum** and the compounding element 'macro-' (as in Macro-Penutian, Macro-Siouan etc.). The proposed distant genetic relationships are much debated. Some scholars employ 'stock' or 'phylum' in the sense of a language family that is large enough to include well-defined or older subfamilies; however, this usage is often confused with the more common employment of these terms for undemonstrated hypotheses of remote linguistic affiliation, making the use of these terms controversial and often confusing. See also **classification of languages, macro-family, subgrouping**.

language maintenance (opposite of **language shift**)   Situation in which a community retains its original language, continues to use its language in face of pressure from a more dominant or prestigious language to shift. See also **endangered language, language shift**.

language shift (opposite of **language maintenance**)   Process in which a community loses its original language and shifts to another, more dominant or prestigious language. The process is often gradual, occurring over generations, resulting in **language death** if the process is completed. See also **endangered language, language death, language maintenance**.

language spread   see **language dispersal**

laryngeal theory   The discovery that **Proto-Indo-European**, by the most probable **reconstruction**, had a series of 'laryngeal' sounds (glottal stops, some fricatives and pharyngeals), retained as such in **Hittite** (and Luwian, also **Anatolian**) but lost, leaving varying impacts on adjacent vowels, in the other branches of the family. The origin of the laryngeal theory is often attributed to the Swiss linguist Ferdinand de Saussure and his essay *Memoire sur le système des voyelles dans les langues indo-européenes* (in 1879), in which, through **internal reconstruction** applied to a series of phonological and morphological alternations in the daughter languages of Proto-Indo-European, he postulated that there must have previously been a set of consonants (de Saussure's *coéfficients sonantiques*) absent except in some of the vowel reflexes of most **Indo-European** languages. In 1929, more concrete evidence of the consonants postulated for the proto-language by de Saussure were found to occur in Hittite cognates with other Indo-European languages. There are varying views on the number of original laryngeals and on their phonetic nature, but three are widely accepted, symbolized as h_1 (neutral, usually resulting in *e*), h_2 '*a*-coloring', and h_3 'o-coloring'. The h_2 '*a*-coloring' laryngeal changed a Proto-Indo-European vowel **e* to *a*, as seen in: Proto-Indo-European **h_2enti* 'before, against', which gave Hittite *hanti* and Latin *ante*; **h₃* 'o-coloring' changed **e* to *o*, as in Proto-Indo-European **h₃ewi-* 'sheep', giving Luwian *hawi-*, Latin *ovis*. In the other branches of Indo-European, these laryngeals after vowels generally resulted in loss of the laryngeal with lengthening of the preceding vowel. See also **ablaut**, **Anatolian**.

law   see **sound law**

laxing   A **sound change** in which a vowel becomes lax, loses tensing. The opposite of laxing is **tensing**. (In comparison with tense sounds, lax sounds are produced with less effort of the vocal tract and less movement and are relatively shorter.) (Also a synchronic phonological process.)

learned loan   A loan into a language from a prestigious, usually literary, ancestor language that is no longer spoken but is well attested (for example, Latin, Greek, Sanskrit). In some cases, where a word has undergone the expected historical development in the language and then, later, that language has borrowed a learned loan from the same source word in the classical language, the result is a pair or words referred to as an **etymological doublet**. This is seen, for example, with Latin *fragilis* 'breakable', the source of both *fragile* and *frail* in French (which gave us the two loanwords in English), where *frail* underwent the regular **sound changes**, for example deletion of intervocalic *g* and loss of final *e*, while *fragile* was a later borrowing back into French from Latin. Other examples include Latin *capital* > Spanish *capital*, *caudal* 'abundant amount', *caudillo* 'leader, headman, dictator, *cabeza* 'head'; Latin *limpidu-* > *límpido* 'limpid', *limpio* 'clean'; *populu-* > Spanish *popular*, *populacho* 'rabble', *pueblo* 'people, town'; Latin *opera* 'work' > *opera* 'opera'; *obra* 'work'; Latin *mixta* 'mixed'

(f) > *mixta* 'mixed' (f), *mesta* 'mixed herd', *mesteño* 'mustang', *mestizo* 'mixed race'; Latin *oculu-* 'eye' > *ocular*, *oculista* 'oculist', *ojo* [óxo] 'eye'. See also **borrowing, hypercorrection, loanword.**

lect   Any clearly identifiable linguistic **variety** (regional dialect, sociolect, idiolect etc.). See also **dialect.**

Lencan   A small **language family** of two **languages**, both now **extinct**, Honduran Lenca and Chilanga or Salvadoran Lenca. Hypotheses have attempted to link Lencan with various other languages in broader genetic groupings, but none has much support. The often repeated hypothesis of a connection between Lencan and **Xinkan** has no reliable evidence and is now abandoned.

lengthening   **Sound change** in which some sound, usually a vowel, is lengthened. See also **compensatory lengthening.**

lenition (also called **weakening**)   **Sound change** in which the resulting sound after the change is conceived of as somehow weaker in articulation than the original sound before the change. Lenitions typically include changes of stops or affricates to fricatives, of two consonants to one, of full consonants to glides (*j* or *w*), sometimes of voiceless consonants to voiced ones in various environments, as well as the complete loss of sounds, among other examples. An example of lenition is the change of the intervocalic stops that were voiceless in Latin (*p, t, k*) to voiced stops (*b, d, g*) in Spanish, as in *skōpa* (spelled *scopa*) > *eskoba* [spelled *escoba*] 'broom', *natāre* > *nadar* 'to swim', *amīka* > *amiga* 'female friend'. The opposite of lenition is **fortition** (**strengthening**). (Lenition is also a synchronic phonological process.)

leveling   see **analogic leveling**

lexical borrowing   see **borrowing, language contact, loan-word**

lexical change   Any change in the lexicon. Also, in a more restricted sense, **lexical replacement**, where one lexical item is replaced by another, either entirely or in its meaning only (with or without **borrowing**). For example, Old English *andwlita* 'face' was replaced by *face* (< French *face*) and Old English *deer* '(generic) animal'> *deer* 'deer', a shift in meaning (compare the German cognate *Tier* 'animal', which did not undergo the change).

lexical diffusion   Gradual spread of a **sound change** from word to word through the lexicon. Lexical diffusion of sound change contrasts with the **Neogrammarian** view that sound change is implemented mechanically, affecting every instance of a sound regardless of the particular words in which the sound is found, and thus considered regular. Lexical diffusion is similar to the Neogrammarian's '**dialect borrowing**', only with some words borrowing from others in the same dialect. Lexical diffusion constitutes a claim about how sound changes are transmitted. (Wang 1969; Chen and Wang 1975; Labov 1994; compare Campbell 2004: 222–4).

Nevertheles, few cases of lexical diffusion have actually been reported. Most **historical linguists** have not been convinced that lexical diffusion occurs. They see the purported cases as being better explained as the results of dialect borrowing, **analogy** and erroneous analysis. Most cases proved not to be real instances of lexical diffusion but to be more reliably explained by other means. For example, important phonetic environments were missed in several of the cases for which lexical diffusion was claimed. In several instances more detailed studies of the same cases have found sounds behaving regularly in change in these environments and no evidence of lexical conditioning. When the environments are understood, **Neogrammarian regularity** was behind the changes, not lexical diffusion. In the examples from the history of Chinese, which had been influential support for the notion of lexical diffusion, the extent of **borrowing** from literary Chinese into the varieties of Chinese studied was much more extensive than originally thought (see **learned loans**); they were just dialect borrowing, which proponents of lexical diffusion later called 'intimate borrowing'; these cases were a misreading of the influence of stylistic choices, **language contact** and sociolinguistic conditions in general (Labov 1994: 444–71).

Labov has attempted to reconcile the mostly regular changes with the few that seem to affect some lexical items but not others. He noted that 'earlier stages of change are quite immune to such irregular lexical reactions [as in lexical diffusion]; and even in a late stage, the unreflecting use of the vernacular preserves that regularity' (Labov 1994: 453). This he calls '**change from below**' – below the level of awareness. Only in later stages of a change do speakers become aware of the change and give it sociolinguistic value (positive or negative) and this often involves the social importance of individual words. Change of this sort is what Labov calls '**change from above**'. Labov believes that lexical diffusion can involve only the later stages of change and change from above, the same kinds of change that are often characterized by **dialect mixture** and **analogical change**, with a higher degree of social awareness or of borrowing from another **dialect** system (Labov 1994: 542–3). See also **regularity hypothesis**.

lexical reconstruction   see **comparative method, reconstruction**

lexicalization   There are a number of definitions of lexicalization, referring to a range of things, all of which loosely have to do with something new or different being added to the lexicon of a language. 'Lexicalization turns linguistic material into lexical items, and renders them still more lexical' (Wischer 2000). Lexicalization typically involves the development of new monomorphemic, non-compositional elements belonging to major lexical classes. For some, lexicalization refers to the process by which anything comes to be outside the productive rules of grammar (and hence mentioned in lexical entries). Thus, 'a sign is lexicalized if it is withdrawn from analytic access and is inventorized'. (The grammar is concerned with signs formed regularly and handled analytically; the lexicon is concerned with signs formed irregularly and handled holistically' (Lehmann 2003). For some scholars, lexicalization is only a **diachronic** process, a kind of **language change**; for others it can also be **synchronic** (involving derivation and word formation). In another view, '**Lexicalization** bleeds grammatical compositions and feeds the lexicon; **grammaticalization** bleeds the lexicon and feeds grammar' (Moreno Cabrera 1998).

Any of the following fall under lexicalization as defined by some, though some definitely are outside lexicalization as seen by others: (1) *Word formation*; some exclude word formation because it is not outside the rules of grammar. (2) **Conversion** (grammatical > lexical), change of something more grammatical to something with more lexical content, for example, the preposition *out* to a verb: *to out someone* 'to reveal someone's secret identity, especially of homosexuals'.

Cases of conversion are controversial, since they are counterexamples to the claim of **unidirectionality** in **grammaticalization**. (3) *Syntactic construction* > *lexeme*, for example *never + the + less* > *nevertheless*, traditionally called **amalgamation**. (4) *Bound morpheme* > *lexeme*, for example, *isms, bi, ex, teen, -gate*; these are also counterexamples to unidirectionality of grammaticalizaton. (5) *Idiomaticization*, loss of semantic compositionality, as in *blackmail*, whose meaning now has nothing to do with 'black' or 'mail'. (6) *Semanticization*, incorporation of inferred meanings into conventional meaning of words, for example, *supposed to* 'presumed to' > 'probably is' > 'should'. (7) *Compounding*, as in *airhead, cashflow*. (8) **Blending**, for example, *workaholic, chocaholic, mochaccino, cyberccino*. See also **amalgamation**.

lexicostatistics The statistical manipulation of lexical material for historical inferences. Lexicostatistics is often used as a synonym for **glottochronology**, though in a more technical sense, lexicostatistics need not be concerned with dating, as glottochronology is.

limitations of (or **constraints** on) **the comparative method** see **time-depth ceiling**

lingua franca (literally, *Frankish tongue)* An inter-ethnic and international, medieval trade *jargon* of the eastern Mediterranean, probably of Italian origin, though its name alludes to a significant contribution by crusaders from the West (known generically as *Franks*, though only some were actually French). The crusader jargon including linguistic elements from **koiné** Greek, Arabic, French and Italian dialects. In modern times, the term is applied to any **language** (mixed or otherwise) that serves as a means of communication across national and ethnic boundaries, for example, French across the many languages in former French colonies of Africa and the Pacific; Arabic across Muslim regions of the Near East and north Africa. English is very widespread as a lingua franca in the world today.

linguistic acculturation   Response in a language to new items that become known through cultural contact. As the speakers of a language in contact with other cultures encounter new cultural items, they may: (1) **borrow** (or import, transfer) the associated vocabulary from that community's language, (2) **innovate** terms from resources internal to their own language, (3) shift the meaning of already existing, native vocabulary (**semantic shift**), including sometimes total displacing an old referent with a new one, or there may be *semantic extension* of an original meaning to encompass a new referent etc. A semantic shift may be combined with some innovated material, so that a borrowed term is modified by a native one. In Kiliwa (**Yuman** family, Baja California, Mexico), contact with Spanish led to many examples that illustrate these acculturating mechanisms. The language initially borrowed a small number of lexical items, for example Spanish *fraile* 'friar' > *paa ʔiy liʔ* 'friar' (lit. 'person (with) tonsured hair'). In contrast to the scarcity of borrowed terms, there is an abundant innovated vocabulary reflecting various stages of technological and cultural influence: *miy kʷxʔaly* 'Hispanic' (lit. 'feet smooth'), *xaʔl kʷñmatp* 'Anglos' (lit. 'water-in dwelling, sailor'). More recent innovations are: *waʔ kʷsʔhin* 'automobile' (lit. 'house running'), *waʔ kʷiʔhiw* 'airplane' (lit. 'house flying'); *qhaay smaa* 'money, metal' (lit. 'cliff root'), *qhaay smaa waʔ* 'bank' (lit. 'money house'), *qhaay smaa kʷxwit* 'banker' (lit. 'money seller').

Examples of **semantic shift** are: the displacement of the aboriginal referent of *xmaʔ* 'quail' > 'poultry'; the subsequent modification of the 'new' term for the original native referent: *xmaʔ piyl tkʷyaq* 'quail; wild poultry' (lit. 'poultry in the wasteland thing dwelling'); *ʔmuw* 'mountain sheep' > (domestic) sheep'; *ʔmuw piyl tkʷyaq* 'mountain sheep, wild sheep' (lit. 'sheep in the wasteland thing dwelling'); *ʔxaq* 'deer' > beef (cattle); *xaq piyl tkʷyaq* 'deer; wild beef' (lit. 'cattle in the wasteland thing dwelling'; Mixco 1977, 1983, 1985, 2000a, 2000b). See also **language contact**.

linguistic archaeology   see **linguistic paleontology, linguistic prehistory**

linguistic area (sometimes also called **Sprachbund, diffusion area, adstratum** and **convergence area**)   A geographical area in which, owing to **language contact** and **borrowing**, languages of a region come to share certain structural features – not only borrowed words, but also shared elements of sound and grammar. **Areal linguistics** is about linguistic areas, some of the best known of which are the **Balkan linguistic area**, *Baltic linguistic area*, **Ethiopian linguistic area, Mesomerican linguistic area, Northwest Coast** (of North America) **linguistic area**, and the **South Asian (or Indian subcontinent) linguistic area**.

linguistic homeland (also called *Urheimat* from the German equivalent)   The geographical location where a **proto-language** was spoken. There are two principal techniques for attempting to determine the location of the original homelands of speakers of **proto-languages**. For the first, a vocabularly-based approach, reconstructed lexical items are sought that are ecologically or geographically diagnostic for a particular region (such as terms for fauna, flora, topography etc.). Clues from terms for fauna and flora should be of the type that several reconstructed plant and animal names converge in particular region to the exclusion of other regions (see **Wörter und Sachen**). Collaboration between paleo-climatologists, paleo-botanists and paleo-zoologists ensures that the plant and animal ranges or ecological niches reflect the approximate time-depth of the proto-language. Terms relating to bodies of water, streams and landforms can also be useful. The greater the variety, intractability and detail of these, the more likely the site is to be an original homeland. Archaeology can assist in identifying material remains that coincide with con-clusions reached independently about the proto-culture and homeland.

The second technique, **linguistic migration theory**, looks at the **classification** (**subgrouping**) of a family and the geographical distribution of its languages, and, rely-ing on notions of *maximum diversity* and *minimum moves*, hypothesizes the most likely location of the original homeland. When a **language family** splits up, it is more likely for the various **daughter languages** to stay close to where they began and less likely for them to move far or frequently. Therefore, based on today's geographical distribution of related languages, one hypothesizes how they got where they are and where they came from. The highest branches on a family tree (the earliest splits in the family) reflect the greatest age, and therefore the area with the greatest linguistic *diversity* – that is, with the most representatives of the higher-order **subgroups** – is likely to be the homeland. In this model, one attempts to determine the minimum number of moves that would be required to reverse these migrations or spreads to bring the languages back to the location of maximum diversity of their closest relatives within their individual subgroups, and then to move the various different subgroups back to the location from which their later distribution can be accounted for with the fewest moves. In this way, by combining the location of maximum diversity and the minimum moves to get languages back to the location of the greatest diversity of their nearest relatives, the location of the homeland is postulated.

Caution must be exercised in the search of a linguistic homeland, since, for example, the criterion of maximum diversity could reflect, instead, the geographical convergence of disparate groups from other points of origin rather than reflecting a shared original homeland. Likewise, **lexical reconstructions** must take into account the likelihood of **semantic shifts** and lexical attrition, which disguise original meanings and geographic origins.

linguistic migration theory   see **linguistic homeland, Wörter und Sachen**

linguistic paleontology, linguistic palaeontology   The use of linguistic information (especially lexical) from a language to make inferences about the history, culture, society and environment of the people who spoke the language in prehistoric times. Linguistic paleontology often involves the investigation of reconstructed vocabulary of some **proto-language** for its cultural content and thus for clues about its speakers. For example, a whole complex of terms relating to various domestic animals can be reconstructed to **Proto-Indo-European,** suggesting that speakers of Proto-Indo-European had intimate knowledge of these animals. Sometimes used as a synonym for **linguistic prehistory.** See also **Wörter und Sachen.**

linguistic prehistory Broadly speaking, linguistic prehistory uses historical linguistic findings for cultural and historical inferences. It correlates information from historical linguistics with information from archaeology, ethnohistory, history, ethnographic analogy, human biology and other sources of information on a people's past in order to obtain a more complete picture of the past. Information from the **comparative method, linguistic homeland** and **linguistic migration theory**, cultural inventories from reconstructed vocabularies of **proto-languages**, **loanwords**, place names, **classification of languages**, **internal reconstruction, dialect** distributions and the like can all provide valuable historical information useful to linguistic prehistory. Linguistic prehistory is also sometimes, misleadingly, called **linguistic paleontology, linguistic archaeology**, and **applied historical linguistics**.

litotes (from Greek *litótēs* 'smoothness, plainness') Exaggeration by understatement (such as 'of no small importance' when 'very important' is meant). A type of **semantic change** resulting from exaggeration by understatement, as for example, English *kill*, which originally meant 'to strike, hit'; saying *hit* but intending it to mean 'kill', is an understatement. See also **hyperbole**.

loan see **loanword**

loan translation see **calque**

loanword (also **loan word**) A word in a language that is borrowed from another language, or, more specifically, a word or expression in a **recipient language** that through the process of **borrowing** has been *borrowed, imported* or *copied* from a **donor language** through bilingual usage during **language contact**. For example, English *pork* is a loanword from French *porc* 'pork', and was not a word in the English language until after it was taken over from French. Loanwords may undergo varying degrees of **naturalization** in their **accommodation** of the phonological, morphological, syntactic or semantic patterns of the recipient language, and may reveal patterned deviations from native structure that can serve as clues to their foreign origin and even their specific original source when the **comparative method** is applied. See also **areal linguistics, learned loan.**

long-range comparison   see **distant genetic relationship**

long-ranger   Someone who favors long-range comparisons, that is, proposals of **distant genetic relationship**. The term is somewhat playful and informal (based on the occasional folk-etymologized version of the name of the 'Lone Ranger' of radio, movie, and television fame), but is also used sometimes in technical linguistic writing.

look-alike (also **lookalike**)   A form in one language that is similar in phonetic shape and meaning to a form in another language, though the similarity may be for-tuitous. Accidentally similar words are often listed as evidence in claims of **distant genetic relationship,** though they are usually not accepted by skeptics unless the simi-larity can be shown somehow to reflect systematic sound correspondences. One major criticism of **multilateral comparison** is that it relies almost exclusively on look-alikes without determining whether the similarity among the compared forms may be due to accident, **borrowing** or other non-inherited factors.

loss   Linguistic change in which linguistic material (a sound, word, construction) is eliminated from its language, due either to deletion of the material from the language or, less frequently, to the material being so changed that it is no longer identified with the source material from which it is derived. Loss is especially associated with the kind of **sound change** in which a sound is subject to either (1) deletion, so that after the change there is nothing where the sound was before the change, or (2) ceases to be distinct in the language because of **merger** with some other sound.

lumper (the opposite of **splitter**) Linguist favorably disposed towards **distant genetic relationships**, towards grouping together languages not yet known to be related to one another in larger unsubstantiated proposals of linguistic kinship, so-called **macro-families**, often on the basis of inconclusive evidence; linguist who engages in making hypotheses of distant genetic relationship.

luxury loan (also called **prestige loan**) This type of **loanword** occurs when, for reasons of **prestige**, a language borrows a word or expression from another language though a viable native word already exists. Thus, French *soirée* 'evening party' and *cuisine* 'kitchen, cooking' entered English meaning 'evening party' and '(fine) cooking', respectively. Similarly, in Middle English, Norman French furnished such terms as: *veal, beef, mutton, pork, poultry*, replacing or competing with native terms for kinds of meat: *calf, cow, lamb, swine, fowl*, respectively in this context.

M

macro- A compounding element used in the names of proposed **distant genetic relationships**, such as in

Macro-Penutian, Macro-Siouan etc., roughly equivalent to **phylum**. See also **macro-family**.

macro-family   A speculative, and often controversial, proposed genetic grouping of languages thought to be distantly related to one another, often on the basis of inconclusive evidence. Campbell (2004: 187–8) finds the term to be superfluous, preferring the term **language family** for those classifications for which there is a broad consensus, with the designation 'proposed **distant genetic relationship**' more accurate for proposed macro-families.

Macro-Gê (Macro-Je)   A proposed **distant genetic relationship** composed of several language families and isolates, many now extinct, along the Atlantic coast (primarily of Brazil). These include Chiquitano, Bororoan, Botocudoan, Rikbaktsa, the Gê family proper, Jeikó, Kamakanan, Maxakalían, Purian, Fulnío, Ofayé and Guató. Many are sympathetic to the hypothesis and several of these languages will very probably be demonstrated to be related to one another eventually, though others will probably need to be separated out (Kaufman 1990, 1994, Rodrigues 1986).

Macro-Guaicuruan (also spelled **Macro-Waykuruan, Macro-Waikuruan**)   A proposed **distant genetic relationship** that would join the *Guaicuruan* and **Matacoan** families of the Gran Chaco in South America in a larger-scale genetic classification. Grammatical similarities, for example in the pronominal systems, have suggested the relationship to some scholars, but the extremely limited lexical evidence raises doubts for others. Some would also add Charruan and Mascoyan to these in an even larger 'Macro-Waikuruan cluster' (Kaufman 1990, 1994).

Macro-Mayan   A proposed **distant genetic relationship** that would join **Mayan, Mixe-Zoquean** and *Totonacan* – in some earlier versions also *Huave* – in a larger genetic grouping. There is some sympathy for this possibility, though it is extremely difficult to distinguish what may be diffused (and thus not evidence of a genetic relationship) from what may possibly be inherited (evidence of the proposed relationship). The hypothesis, though plausible, does not have sufficient evidence for it to be embraced (see Campbell 1997: 323–4).

Macro-Penutian   see **Penutian**

Macro-Siouan   A proposed **distant genetic relationship** that would join **Siouan** with either **Iroquoian** or **Caddoan** or both. It has some supporters, though most discount the hypothesis as not having sufficient evidence in support (Chafe 1976; see Campbell 1997: 262–9 for a critical evaluation).

Maiduan   A small family of languages in northern California, with Maidu, Nisenan and Konkow. Maiduan was among the original Californian groups postulated to belong to the hypothesized but disputed **Penutian macro-family**.

maintenance   see **language maintenance**

Maipurean, Maipuran   An alternate name for the **Arawakan** language family. Some scholars prefer Maipurean or Maipuran for the name of the family of languages that are known to be related, reserving

Arawakan as the designation for a possibly broader grouping that would include the languages known to be related, the 'Maipurean' languages, as well as, possibly, some other languages and **language families** not yet clearly demonstrated as belonging to the family.

majority-wins   A principle or rule of thumb in **reconstruction** by the **comparative method** that, unless there is evidence to the contrary, the sound or morpheme or construction that is attested in the majority of the **daughter languages** should be chosen as the reconstructed proto-form. The rationale for following the majority-wins principle is that it is less likely that several languages will have undergone a particular change to end up with the same sound in a set of sound correspondence or the same morpheme or construction independently; elements shared by several languages are likely to be preserved and unchanged from the **proto-language** rather than to be the result of several independent changes.

The majority-wins principle is especially common in reconstruction of sounds. Some sound changes are so common and languages undergo them independently with such ease that several related languages might undergo one of these kind of changes independently of each other, giving a majority in a sound correspondence set that is due to change and not to direct inheritance. It is also possible that all the daughter languages may undergo changes so that none reflects the proto sound unchanged. Also, majority rule may not work as well if some of the languages are more closely related to one another than others: if some of the languages belong to the same **branch** (**subgroup**) of the family then they have a more immediate ancestor, which itself is a daughter of the proto language (see **language families**). This intermediate language could have undergone a change that it passed on directly to its daughters when they were formed, and each of these would then inherit the changed sound that their immediate common ancestor had undergone. This could mean that a number of languages from one subgroup could share a change and thus exhibit a different **correspondence** from that of languages from other groups. In this way, if a particular subgroup happened to have a number of daughter languages, the sound represented by the languages of that particular subgroup could seem to be in the majority, when, in fact, they represent but one vote, that of the immediate ancestor that underwent the change reflected in its multiple daughters. Thus, care must be exercised in interpreting majority wins.

mama–papa vocabulary   see **nursery word**

markedness and language change   The theory of markedness originated with the *Prague school* in the early twentieth century and was further refined and promoted by *generative* linguists. Markedness is based on the observation that some linguistic elements and structures in language are more natural, more expected, more frequent across languages, easier for children to acquire in child language acquisition, last lost in language pathologies and more common as the outcome of linguistic changes – these are called *unmarked*. On the other hand, other elements and structures are less natural, unexpected, less frequent across languages, more difficult to acquire in child language acquisition, lost earlier in language pathologies and less likely as the outcome of linguistic changes – these are called *marked*. **Historical linguistics**, through the study of **language change**, both contributes to the understanding of markedness and often utilizes it to determine the best hypotheses of change and reconstruction. See **directionality, naturalness, typology.**

mass comparison   An older term for **multilateral comparison.**

Matacoan-Waykuruan (Guaycuruan)   see **Macro-Guaicuruan**

maximum differentiation   The notion that the sounds in a phonological system tend to be distributed so as to allow as much perception difference between them as the articulatory space can provide. Thus, if a language has only three vowels it is expected that they will be spread out, often with *i* (high front unrounded), *u* (high back rounded) and *a* (low central or back unrounded); we do not expect them to be bunched up in articulatory space, say, all in the high front area (say, *i, I* and *y*). This belief is confirmed by the languages of the world, in which most of the three-vowel systems have /i, u, a/ or /i, o, a/. If a language has four stops, we do not expect them to be bunch at one point of articulation, say all labials (*p, b, p', pʰ*) with none at other points of articulation; rather, we expect them to be spread across labial, alveolar, velar and other points of articulation. (See Martinet 1970.) Maximum differentiation is often hypothesized as an underlying motivation in **chain shifts**, specifically in **push chains.**

Mayan   A family of some thirty languages in Guatemala, Mexico and adjacent regions. Some of the better-known Mayan languages are Huastec, Yucatec (Yucatec Maya), K'iche', Kaqchikel, Q'eqchi', Mam, Chol and several others. The Mayan hieroglyphic inscriptions were written mostly in Cholan; the later hieroglyphic codices were written in Yucatec. Proto-Mayan is well reconstructed; its homeland is postulated to have been in the Cuchumatanes mountains of Guatemala around 4,200 years ago.

Mayan-Araucanian   A discarded proposal of **distant genetic relationship** that would group **Mayan** and *Araucanian* (**Mapudungu**) of South America together (Stark 1970).

Maya-Chipayan   A discarded proposal of **distant genetic relationship** that would group **Mayan** and *Uru-Chipaya* of Bolivia together (Olson 1964, 1965; see Campbell 1973 for evaluation).

Maya-Chipayan-Yungan   A discarded proposal of **distant genetic relationship** that would group Olson's proposed but now abandonded **Maya-Chipayan** hypothesis with *Yungan* of Peru (Stark 1972).

mechanisms of (language) change   Fundamental principles of **language change** embodying the motivation for the language changes they govern and help to explain. For example, it is argued that there are only three mechanisms of **syntactic change: reanalysis, extension** and **borrowing.**

mechanisms of syntactic change   There are three principal mechanisms of syntactic change: **reanalysis, extension** and **borrowing.** Reanalysis arises from the potential for more than one analysis of a given construction. Extension extends a pattern emerging through reanalysis beyond the contexts in which it originated to new ones. Syntactic borrowing accounts for how one language imports grammatical morphemes and constructions from another.

In reanalysis, a change occurs in some aspect of the underlying structure without affecting its surface manifestation. An example in English of how the potential for more than one reading can lead to reanalysis is seen in constructions with the verb to *go*, for example, *going to* as a verb of motion (as in *I'm going to town*) acquired the additional interpretation of a future marker, as in *I'm going to marry her*, making it a new auxiliary verb.

Extension, after reanalysis, changes the surface manifestation without affecting the underlying structure. The reanalyzed *going to* as a future marker (from a motion verb) was extended to occur with all infinitive complements, whereas, before, it was limited to complements that could occur with *go* as a verb of motion; hence, after the extension, but not before, examples such as the following are possible: *she is going to go over there*, *she is going to like cabbage*, *it is going to rain* etc.

Linguists have come to understand that **syntactic borrowing** is more frequent than it was once thought to be. Pipil (Uto-Aztecan, El Salvador) borrowed a comparative construction from Spanish, as in Spanish *esa mujer es **más** linda **que** tú* [that woman is *more* pretty *than* you] 'that woman is prettier than you', whose equivalent in Pipil, which shows the borrowing, is *ne si:wat Ø **más** gala:na ke taha* [that woman Ø **more** pretty **than** you] 'that woman is prettier than you'.

merger   **Sound change** in which two (or more) distinct sounds fuse into one, leaving fewer phonemes in the phonological inventory than there were before the change. Often the result of merger is that two sounds merge into an existing sound, meaning, essentially, the loss of one of the sounds (as, for example, the change of l^j, j > j in most varieties of Latin American Spanish). Spanish used to contrast the two sounds l^j (palatalized *l*) and *j*, and the contrast is still maintained in some dialects in Spain and in the Andes region of South America and Paraguay; however, in most other dialects, these two sounds merged into one, *j*, as in *calle* /kalʲe/ > /kaje/ 'street', *llamar* /lʲamar/ > /jamar/ 'to call'. Less frequently the result of a merger can be that two (or more) sounds merge into some sound that was not formerly part of the language, as for example in the change in pre-modern northern Spanish: ʦ, ʣ > θ. Another example is the merger of interdental θ and apical alveolar ʂ to dental *s* in southern Spain and Latin American Spanish. For example, *caza* /kaθa/ 'hunt, chase' and *casa* /kaʂa/ 'house' are both /kasa/ in the south of Spain and throughout Latin America.

A linguistic axiom is that *mergers are irreversible*. This means that when sounds have completely merged a subsequent change will not be able to undo the change and restore the original distinctions.

merger, near   see **near merger**

Mesoamerican linguistic area (sometimes **Meso-American linguistics area**)   Linguistically, Mesoamerica is one of the most ancient and diverse culture areas in the western hemisphere. After millennia of contact, the various language isolates and families of the region have come to share a number of traits not found in families immediately outside the area; thus these traits become diagnostic for membership in the **linguistic area**. The language families and isolates of this region are: the Nahua(n) (or Aztecan) branch of Uto-Aztecan, Mixe-Zoquean, Mayan, Xinkan, Otomanguean, Totonacan, Tarascan (or Purépecha), Cuitlatec, Tequistlatecan and Huave. Among the traits that define the area are: (1) Nominal possession of the type: *his-dog the man* 'the man's dog', as in Pipil (Nahuan): *i-pe:lu ne ta:kat* 'his-dog the man'; (2) locative expressions composed of noun roots and possessive pronominal affixes, for example, *my-head* for 'on me', as in Tz'utujil (Mayan): *(č)-r-i:x* [at-**his/her/its**-BACK] 'in back of, behind him/her/it', *(č)-w-i:x* [at-**my**-BACK] 'in back of me, behind me'; (3) vigesimal numeral systems, as seeen in Chol (Mayan): *hun-k'al* '20' (1x20), *čaʔ-k'al* '40' (2x20), *hoʔ-k'al* '100' (5x20), *hun-bahk'* '400'(1-bahk'), *čaʔ-bahk'* '800' (2x400) etc.; (4) general lack of verb-final languages (non-SOV [Subject-Object-Verb]), though SOV orders predominate in the languages immediately to the north and south of the Mesoamerican area; the languages of the Mesoamerican area have VOS (Verb-Object-Subject), VSO (Verb-Subject-Object) or SVO (Subject-Verb-Object) orders; (5) shared loan translations (**calques**) for compounds, including: *boa* = deer-snake, *egg* = bird-stone/bone, *lime* = stone-ash, *knee* = leg-head, *wrist* = hand-neck.

In addition to the above, there are also traits common to the area but that may also occur outside it, and others shared by several languages of the area, but not by all the languages here. (Campbell, Kaufman and Smith-Stark 1986.)

metanalysis (from Greek *meta* 'change' + *analysis* 'analysis' also sometimes called **reanalysis**) Traditionally two things are treated under the heading of metanalysis, **amalgamation** and 'metanalysis proper' (today more often called **reanalysis**). Metanalysis involves a change in the structural analysis, in the interpretation of which phonological material goes with which morpheme in a word or construction, for example, English *adder* is from Old English *næddre*; the change came about through a reinterpretation (reanalysis) of the initial *n-* of the noun as the final -*n* of the article in the article–noun sequence *a* + *nǣddre* > *an* + *adder* (compare the unchanged German cognate *Nater* 'adder, viper').

metaphony   see **umlaut**

metaphor (from Greek *metaphorā*, 'transference' *metapherein* 'to transfer')   **Semantic change** that involves understanding or experiencing one kind of thing in terms of another kind of thing thought to be similar in some way. Metaphor involves extensions in the meaning of a word that suggest a semantic similarity or connection between the new sense and the original one, as in the famous example of English *bead*, now meaning 'small piece of (decorative) material pierced for threading on a line', which comes from Middle English *bede* 'prayer, prayer bead', which in Old English was *beode* 'prayer'. The semantic shift from 'prayer' to 'bead' came about through the metaphoric extension from the 'prayer', which was kept track of by the rosary bead, to the rosary bead itself, and then eventually to any 'bead', even including 'beads' of water.

The term 'metaphor' originates in the conceptual imagery of classical rhetoric, in which a relationship is established between two or more otherwise dissimilar objects, ideas or concepts that are nonetheless perceived to be capable of sharing a (figurative) similarity, as in the expression, the *sky is weeping*. In the domain of semantic change, an extension or transfer of meaning of a word is based on such a similarity bridging the old and new meanings, typically involving a figurative leap across semantic domains. Thus, Latin *pensāre* 'to weigh' > Spanish *pensar* 'to think, (to weigh mentally)'; Latin *captāre* 'to seize' > Spanish *captar* 'to understand' (compare English 'to catch on, to get it'.) Similarly, Latin *folia* 'leaves' > Spanish *hoja* 'leaf' and by metaphor 'sheet of paper', and French *feuille* 'leaf, sheet of paper'; Latin *perna* 'ham' > Spanish *pierna* 'leg'; Latin *testa* 'clay pot' > French *tête* 'head'.

metathesis (from Greek *metaθesis* 'transposition, change of sides')   **Sound change** involving the transposition of sounds; sound change in which sounds exchange positions with one another within a word. For example, [Old English *brid* > Modern English *bird*; Old English *hros* > *horse*.

The change may be **synchronic**, as in Quechan (Yuman): *xmñaaw* ~ *mxñaaw* 'shoe'; Spanish (non-standard varieties) *ciudad* 'city' [sjuðá(ð) ~ swiðá(ð)], or **diachronic**, as in German *Brunnen* ~ *Born* 'well, spring, fountain'. Spanish loanwords phonologically **naturalized** in American Indian languages occasionally undergo metathesis; for example, New Mexico Tewa: *bíhera* < *virgen* 'virgin'; Acoma: *sawarníísku* < *San Francisco* 'St Francis'.

metatypy   Associated with Malcolm Ross (1996, 1997), extreme change due to **language contact** in which the structure of a language is thoroughly changed to be more similar to that of a neighboring language. Ross found that the grammar of Takia (**Austronesian** language of Papua New Guinea) was changed to match exactly the structure of the grammar of neighboring Waskia (**Papuan** language) in morpheme by morpheme translations of sentences. Equated with **extreme structural borrowing** (Thomason and Kaufman 1988).

metonymy (from Greek *metōnomia* 'name transformation, name change')   **Semantic change** in which a word comes to include additional senses that were not originally present but that are closely associated with the word's original meaning, although the conceptual association between the old and new meanings may not be precise. Metonymic changes typically involve contiguity – a shift in meaning from one thing to another that is present in the context, for example, English *cheek* 'fleshy side of the face below the eye', which in Old English meant 'jaw, jawbone'. This term originates in the conceptual imagery of classical rhetoric, involving an exchange or substitution of one term for another (sometimes, by semantic extension, to include the meaning of the second term), for example German *stillen* 'to silence' > 'to nurse (an infant)'. The original terms usually share little directly in common semantically (see **synecdoche**). Thus, *one drinks a glass* meaning the *contents* of the glass or *one reads Shakespeare* meaning *a work* by him, one says *the White House issued a disclaimer* actually meaning the *President* or a *presidential spokesperson* did so.

In semantic change, it is not always easy to distinguish the domains of **metaphor** and metonymy. For example, either can easily accommodate the following example: Middle English *bede* 'prayer, petition' > *(rosary) bead* > *(generic) bead* (including *bead of perspiration*). Other examples are: Latin *maxilla* 'jaw' > Spanish *mejilla* 'cheek', Latin *cathedra* 'chair, seat' > Old Spanish *cadera(s)* 'buttocks' > Modern Spanish *cadera(s)* 'hips'.

Miao-Yao (also called **Hmong-Mien**)   A **language family** spoken by the Miao and Yao peoples of southern China and Southeast Asia. Some proposals would classify Miao-Yao with **Sino-Tibetan**, others with **Tai** or **Austronesian**; none of these has much support.

Mixe-Zoquean   A family of languages spoken in southern

Mexico. The Mixean branch includes the Mixe languages of Oaxaca along with Sayula Popoluca and Oluta Popoluca of Veracruz; the Zoque branch includes the Zoque languages of Chiapas, Oaxaca and Tabasco as well as Sierra Popoluca and Texistepec Popoluca in Veracruz. Mixe-Zoquean has been hypothesized to be part of the broader **Macro-Mayan** hypothesis (with **Mayan** and *Totonacan*), though it has not been possible to confirm this hypothesis. It is argued that the bearers of Olmec civilization, the first highly successful agricultural civilization of Mesoamericia, spoke a Mixe-Zoquean language (Campbell and Kaufman 1976).

mixed language (sometimes the German **Mischsprache** is also used in English)   A language that does not have a single ancestor but, rather, is composed of the fusion of large amounts of grammatical and lexical material from two or more languages. Mixed languages do not arise in the normal fashion by descent from a single parent language through language diversification, and therefore mixed languages constitute problems for **language classification** and for assumptions about how **genetic relationships** among languages can be determined. An often-cited example of such a language is *Michif* spoken by the *Métis* people of North America (mostly Canada). Spoken by an ethnic group that combines French-Canadian with Cree (Algonquian) ethnic and cultural heritage, the language is a fusion of French nominal morpho-syntax with a Cree verbal system. Other mixed languages include Ma'a (Bantu-Cushitic) in East African, and Copper Island (or Mednyj) Aleut (Russian-Aleut) in Alaska. Sometimes the German *Mischsprache* is also used in English.

Modern   Placed before a language name, 'Modern' indicates the form of the language known in the most recent or current period of its history, as in **Modern English**. It is often used to distinguish modern varieties of a language from older attested stages in the language's history, for example distinguishing Modern English from Old English, Middle English and Early Modern English.

Mongolian   A family of languages spoken by about 6 million people in the Republic of Mongolia, in the Inner Mongolian Autonomous Region of China and in the Lake Baykal region of Siberia, with some speakers in the Xinjiang Uygur Autonomous Region and Manchuria, in China. Some Mongolian languages are Kalmyck, Buryat and Khalkha. Mongolian is often believed to belong to the much disputed **Altaic** proposed **distant genetic relationship**, though a majority of specialists now reject the Altaic hypothesis.

Mon-Khmer   A **language family** of southeast Asia, thought by many to be a branch of the proposed larger **Austroasiatic** family, together with the **Munda** languages of India. The Mon-Khmer languages include Cambodian (or Khmer), Mon (or Talaing), Vietnamese, Nicobarese and numerous others.

monogenesis   Single origin of human language, or of a particular language.
    Perhaps most linguists believe that monogenesis is possible, that true human language emerged only once in humankind's early past, that there was a single original human language from which all other later languages have developed. Supporters of **Proto-World** (**global etymologies**) are committed to monogenesis. The opposite of monogenesis is **polygenesis**, the theory that the breakthrough to human language could have taken place

independently more than once in different places or times. At present it is impossible to know whether the monogenesis or polygenesis view is correct – both are possible. Some scholars favor monogenesis on the basis of parsimony alone, that less is required for language to have emerged once than for it to have emerged more than once from the set of circumstances pertaining immediately before human language developed.

In a different sense monogenesis was favored by some as their explanation for similarities found among many **creole** languages. They hypothesized that there was a single original **pidgin** language that began with *Sabir* (the original lingua franca of the crusaders), which was carried aboard ships to become a Portuguese-based *nautical pidgin* and then developed further in the context of the West African slave trade as it passed on to slaves both in transport from Africa and on plantations where it was then relexified as Portuguese words were replaced by words from the dominant languages of the plantations (English in English-based creoles, French in French-based creoles and so on). The monogenesis hypothesis of creole origins holds that all creole languages developed in this way from the single original pidgin. In contrast, **polygenesis** theories of pidgin origins assume that the development of a pidgin in one community may be independent of the development of a pidgin in another, and that structural similarities among pidgins and creoles worldwide are due to the fact that similar languages were involved (European and West African) and to similar processes of simplification that these underwent. Monogenesis theories assume the diffusion of a single pidgin to other areas via travel and migration. For **varieties** lexically based on Spanish, English, Dutch and French, **relexification** from the original Portuguese source was assumed. Monogenesis for pidgin–creole origins is mostly rejected now, since it would exclude all pidgins and creoles not based on European languages, for example Chinook Jargon, based primarily on Native American languages of the Northwest Coast.

monophthongization   Sound change in which two members of a *diphthong* or members of a vowel cluster are reduced to a simple single vowel, to only one vocalic articulatory gesture (a monophthong), either in the coalescence of its members or by the loss of one member of a diphthong. Example of monophthongization through coalescence of the parts of a diphthong are Latin *aurum* 'gold' > Spanish *oro*, Old Spanish *fablarai* 'I shall speak' > *(h)ablaré*; and Middle High German *guot* > German *gut* 'good'. Examples of monophthongization via loss of one of the vocal element from a diphthong are: Old Spanish *castiella* *[kastjélʲa] > Modern Spanish *castilla* [kastílʲa] 'castle'. Some **Romance** languages show the rise of diphthongs from Latin, through **metathesis**, with subsequent monophthongization in some of the languages: Latin *sapui* 'I knew' > Early Ibero-Romance *saube* (see Portuguese *soube*), but this *au* diphthong was monophthongized in Spanish *supe* (with learned restoration of the Latin medial consonant).

morphological change   Any historical change that affects the morphological structure of a language (for a review of types of morphological change, see Andersen 1980).

morphological conditioning   (also called **grammatical conditioning**)   Non-phonetic properties in the environments in which a **sound change** takes place. A sound change is said to be morphologically or grammatically conditioned when it takes place regularly except in a certain morphological context, or, in another sense, when it takes place in a particular morphological environment rather than a strictly phonological one. A well-known example thought to illustrate morphological conditioning in the former, more general sense is the loss of intervocalic *s* in classical Greek except in certain 'future' and 'aorist' verb forms, in which case the *s* was not lost. Loss of *s* by regular sound change here would have destroyed the phonological form of the 'future' morpheme, -*s*, obliterating it. In the view favoring morphological conditioning, the sound change was prevented in just those cases in which the meaning distinction between 'future' and 'present' would have been lost, and that, they argue, is why intervocalic *s* was morphologically conditioned, not lost, in those 'future' forms. However, the *s* of the 'future' was freely lost in verbs ending in a nasal or a liquid, where the future/present distinction could be signaled formally by the *e* that these future stems take. Thus in *poié-ō* 'I do' / *poié-s-ō* 'I will do' the *s* of the 'future' was maintained, since otherwise the two would be identical and it would not be possible to distinguish the 'present' from the 'future'; however, in *mén-ō* 'I remain' / *mené-ō* [< **mene-s-ō*] 'I will remain' the *s* was lost since the 'future' could be distinguished from the 'present' based on the difference in the stem (*mén-* 'present' / *mené-* 'future').

Not all accept the possibility of morphologically conditioned sound changes; some believe such changes rather reflect **analogy**. In Greek verb roots that end in consonants (other than liquids and nasals) the *s* of 'future' was not threatened, since it was not between vowels, for example *trép-s-ō* 'I will turn' (*trép-ō* 'I turn'). In this view, forms such as *poié-s-ō* are seen as actually at one time having lost the intervocalic *s* that marked 'future' by the regular change, but, later in time, the *s* 'future' was restored by analogy based on the *s* 'future' of consonant-final verbs such as *trép-s-ō*, thus for 'I will do': *poié-s-ō* > *poiéō* by sound change, then *poiéō* > *poié-s-ō* by analogy.

There is another usage of the term 'morphological conditioning', too. In structuralist morphological analysis, morphological conditioning was contrasted with *phonological conditioning* of allomorphs. Allomorphs whose distribution could be accounted for by stating the phonological environments in which they occurred were phonologically conditioned. For example, the -*s* and -*z* allomorphs of English plural are phonologically conditioned, with -*s* when attached to a morpheme ending in a (non-sibilant) voiceless sound and -*z* when attached to a morpheme ending in a (non-sibilant) voiced sound (as in /bets/ 'bets' with -*s* but /bedz/ 'beds' with -*z*). However, with allomorphs -Ø and -*en*, as in *fish*, *sheep*, *deer* (as plurals) and *oxen*, one has to know the morphemes to which these allomorphs are attached to know when they are used, hence morphological conditioning of these allomorphs. Of course, it is possible to write phonological rules to account for the phonetic shape of the phonologically conditioned allomorphs (making the phenomenon part of phonology rather than morphology *per se*), but the morphologically conditioned allomorphs still remain exceptions to such phonological rules and require mention in the rules of the specific morphemes to which they are attached. Of course, these **synchronic** descriptions are the results of changes in the past, both phonological and **analogical**.

morphological reconstruction **Reconstruction** of the inflexional and derivational morphology of a **proto-language** by the **comparative method**. In the course of phonological and lexical reconstruction polymorphemic words are often reconstructed, and standard morphological analysis of these reconstructed proto words provides the proto morphology as a bonus, so to speak. (See **syntactic reconstruction**.)

While, in some situations, this technique can recover a considerable amount of the proto morphology, it works less well where the cognate grammatical morphemes have undergone functional or positional shifts or have been lost due to other changes in the languages. Successful reconstruction here, as with phonological and lexical reconstruction, depends on the nature of the evidence preserved in the languages being compared. For example, in the comparison of the modern **Romance** languages, we are able to recover only some aspects of the morphology of *Proto-Romance* because much has been lost in the various languages; however, in a comparison of nouns in various cases in older **Indo-European** languages, we are able to recover much of the original nominal case system by the comparative method.

Mosan   A now abandoned proposal of **distant genetic relationship** that would group **Salishan**, **Wakashan** and **Chimakuan** together (Sapir 1929, Swadesh 1953a, 1953b).

multilateral comparison (also **mass comparison**)   Approach that attempts to establish **genetic relationships** among languages by relying principally on inspectional resemblances among lexical items in the languages compared. This method, associated with Joseph Greenberg (1963, 1987), is based on **look-alikes** determined by visual inspection, 'looking at ... many languages across a few words' rather than 'at a few languages across many words' (Greenberg 1987: 23), where the shared lexical similarities alone are taken as evidence of genetic relationship. As Newman (2000: 262), a supporter of the method, points out, 'in this method, there is no requirement that regular sound correspondences have been established by the comparative method ... only that words look alike.' As has been repeatedly pointed out, where multilateral comparison stops – after identifying superficial lexical resemblances – is where standard approaches start, since lexical similarities among languages can be due to **borrowing, accident, onomatopoeia** etc., not just to inheritance from a common ancestor. These other possible explanations for the similarities need to be eliminated if a case for genetic relationship is to be believable, and this is not done in multilateral comparison. The premise underlying multilateral comparison is that whenever a number of such similarities occurs a genetic relationship can be inferred. Greenberg allegedly utilized this method for his classification of languages of Africa, of the Pacific (see **Indo-Pacific**) and of the Americas (see **Amerind**), and it is also the method behind **global etymologies**. Most historical linguists reject the method and the proposed genetic relationships based on it. See **distant genetic relationship, Khoisan, Nilo-Saharan, Niger-Kordofanian, macro-family**.

multiple causation   The interaction of more than one *causal factor* to bring about a linguistic change. For example, a particular change in some language may be caused by both the tendency towards **ease of articulation** and influence due to **language contact** working together.

　　The large number of complex and interacting causal factors in language change lead some scholars to believe that it is not possible to 'explain' language change fully, since they equate explanation with prediction, as is required in some approaches to the philosophy of science. However, a more optimistic view is one that looks forward to the identification of the various causal factors and to a rigorous accounting for their complex interaction. (Campbell 2004: 326–9). See also **explanation of linguistic change, external causal factor, internal causal factor**.

Munda   A family of some sixteen languages, mostly spoken in India. Most scholars classify Munda together with **Mon-Khmer** as members of the broader postulated **Austroasiatic** family. Some of the Munda languages are Santhali; Mundari, Sora, Korku etc.

Muskogean A **language family** in the southeastern USA. Muskogean includes: Choctaw, Chickasaw, Creek, Koasati, Mikasuki, Alabama and Appalachee.

mutual intelligibility   Ability of individuals speaking two or more varieties of the same language to communicate with one another without major difficulty. The criterion of mutual intelligibility is often cited as the diagnostic test for the distinction between varieties of the same language (dialects) and distinct languages. This criterion is successful if there is no mutual intelligibility – as would be seen in a clear case of distinct languages. However, on occasion the divergence is incomplete, with **partial intelligibility** and in some cases there is **unidirectional** (non-mutual or non-reciprocal **intelligibility**). This is the case in languages like Spanish and Portuguese: spoken Spanish is intelligible to most Portuguese speakers, but the reverse is not true; Portuguese is not easily intelligible to Spanish speakers.

N

Na-Dené   A disputed proposal of **distant genetic relationship**, put forward by Sapir (1915), that would group *Haida*, *Tlingit* and **Eyak-Athabaskan**. There is considerable disagreement about whether Haida is related to the others. The relationship between Tlingit and Eyak-Athabaskan seems more likely, and some scholars misleadingly use the name 'Na-Dené' to mean a grouping of these two without Haida.

Nahali   A language **isolate** in central India.

Nakh-Dagestan   (also called **Dagestanian, Northeast Caucasian**)   A **language family** of the Caucasus, spoken in the Dagestan, Chechnya and Ingushetia regions of Russia, and in northern Azerbaijan and Georgia. Some languages of the family include: Bats, Ingush, Chechen, Avar, Andi, Tsez, Lak, Lezgian, Archi and Udi, among numerous others. These languages are known from having very complex inventories of consonants.

narrowing   Semantic change (also sometimes called **specialization**, *restriction*) in which the range of meanings is decreased so that there are fewer contexts in which a word can be used appropriately than before the change. An example is *meat*, which originally meant 'food' in general (as in the King James translation of the Bible), which later narrowed its meaning to 'meat' ('food of flesh'). Another example is *hound* 'a species of dog (long-eared hunting dog that follows its prey by sent)' which in its Old English form meant 'dog' in general.

nasal assimilation   A **sound change** (also the name of a **synchronic** phonological process) in which a nasal consonant changes to match the point of articulation of a consonant in its immediate environment. For example, /in-/ the negative prefix of English assimilates to the point of articulation of following stops: [ɪm] *impossible*, [ɪn] *intangible*, [ɪŋ] *incredible* (the English change in /ɪŋ-/ is optional before velars). See also **assimilation**.

nasalization A **sound change** (also the name of a **synchronic** phonological process) in which a sound, typically a vowel, acquires a nasal feature, usually by **assimilation** from a nearby nasal consonant, for example French *bon* 'good' [bõ] and Portuguese *bom* [bõ] (< Latin *bonus* 'good')).

naturalization (also called **accommodation** [of loanwords]) Process by which a borrowed word is adjusted phonologically, morphologically, syntactically or semantically to accommodate the structures of the **recipient language**. In particular, **loanwords** that do not conform to native phonological patterns are modified to fit the sounds and phonological combinations permitted in the borrowing language. In the case of **prestige** or **luxury loans**, naturalization can be minimal or avoided altogether. However, in the case of most loanwords, adjustments can be expected in one or more of the characteristics listed above, especially its phonological form. An example of differing degrees of naturalization in British and North American English is the word *garage* (< French *carriage)*, whereas British pronunciations tend to show a shift from the final-syllable stress of French to the typical first-syllable stress pattern of native English words of this form [gǽrɪǰ], where American pronunciations preserve the final-syllable stress typical of French [garáǰ, garáʒ] often with the less native [ʒ] also. **Mayan** languages do not permit initial consonant clusters, and consequently

Spanish *cruz* /krus/ 'cross' was borrowed as *rus* in Chol (Mayan), in which the initial consonant of the donor form was simply left out, and as *kurus* in Tzotzil (another Mayan language), in which the consonant cluster was interrupted by insertion of a vowel between *k* and *r*.

naturalness (in **language change**)   A linguistic property often invoked as something explaining aspects of language change or of linguistic structure, though rarely defined explicitly. In general, things seen to obtain frequently cross-linguistically, things acquired early in child language acquisition and things resulting frequently in linguistic changes are held to be more natural than less frequent things (things acquired later in first language acquisition and things that rarely result from changes). Naturalness and **markedness** are often equated, with what is less marked being more natural. For example, very frequent changes such as **loss** of vowel length, **nasalization** of vowels before nasal consonants, **palatalization** of velars before front vowels etc. are seen as natural. Unusual changes, such as Nahuatl's change of *t* to *tl* before *a*, are unnatural.

Naturalness plays a role in many aspects of **historical linguistics**. For example, **reconstructions** that are natural (involve no elements that do not typically co-occur in languages) are favored while unnatural ones require much more evidence to be accepted. Postulated **sound changes** in a language that are natural require little defense, but unnatural ones require strong evidence.

near merger (also **near-merger**)   Change in which two sounds become so similar to one another observers claim they have merged although acoustic studies show that words with the different sounds are consistently distinguished. Another interpretation of this term is that it is a partial **merger** that can be distinguished from a complete **merger** in that only the former involves a *conditioned rule*, where the merger takes place in certain environments only. Thus in Uradhi, an Australian language of Northern Queensland, **w* and **p* merge in word-initial position only, as seen in: **pata* 'bite' > *wata*; **pinta* 'arm' > *winta*; **pupu* 'buttock' > *wupu*; **wapun* 'head' > *wapun*; **wujpu* 'old man' > *wujpu* (Crowley 1997: 77–8).

Since true mergers are irreversible, another possible interpretation of this term is that of a false or **apparent merger**. See **reversal of merger**.

neoclassical compound   A compound of which at least one member is a Greek or Latin morpheme, for example, English *auto-*, *bio-*, *mega-*, *trans-* etc., as in, *biodiversity*, *mega-bucks*, *micro-manage* etc. See also **lexical change**, **neologism**.

Neogrammarian hypothesis   see **regularity hypothesis**

Neogrammarians (< German *Junggrammatiker*)   The generation of mostly German **Indo-Europeanists** in the late nineteenth and early twentieth centuries whose ideas became central to historical linguistic thought, particularly those about **sound change**. The Neogrammarians were a group of younger scholars – Karl Brugmann, Berthold Delbrück, August Leskien, Hermann Osthoff, Hermann Paul, and others – who antagonized the leaders of the field by attacking older thinking and loudly proclaiming their own views. They were called *Junggrammatiker* 'young grammarians' by the more established scholars, where *jung-* 'young' had the sense of 'young Turks', originally intended as a humorous and critical nickname, though they took on the name as their own. They defended the principle of **regularity of language change**, also called the **Neogrammarian hypothesis** or the **regularity principle**, which placed sound change beyond the domain of irregularity or unpredictability as an inexorably mechanical process (as reflected in their slogan, '*sound laws suffer no exceptions*', Osthoff and Brugmann 1878). In spite of protests and proposed counterexamples from the then-nascent field of **dialectology**, the dialectologists' slogan that '**every word has its own history**' has done little to shake confidence in the regularity of sound change, and the **comparative method** (which has the regularity of sound change as one of its **basic assumptions**) was successfully applied to an ever-increasing number of **language families** around the globe. In the latter decades of the twentieth century, the field of **sociolinguistics** (see Labov 1994) arose to focus on issues raised by the earlier dialectologists and others regarding the **transition problem** of how sound change takes place in a language and the **language variation** that inevitably accompanies **language change**. While understanding of how sound changes proceed has increased, the Neogrammarian position remains relatively intact. See **lexical diffusion**.

Neolinguistics   A school of linguistics largely opposed to Neogrammarian thinking. It developed in Italy around Matteo Bàrtoli in the early twentieth century and had a large geographical orientation, influenced by Croce's philosophy. Neolinguists favored the view that when different words with similar meaning were distributed among related languages across a large area, those in peripheral areas were likely to be older, those in the center innovations.

neologism (< Greek *neo-* 'new', *logos* 'word'; also called **lexical innovation**)   New **coinages** in a language. These can originate by a variety of not necessarily distinct mechanisms – for example, in the wholesale lexical innovation of new items or expressions; through the **semantic extension** (metaphorical or otherwise) of already existing vocabulary (such as personal names, toponyms, brand names, **acronyms**, compounding etc.); through the **borrowing** of **loanwords** from other languages and so forth. *Slang* is an excellent source for **root creations**, words with no detectible lexical source, such as *zilch*, *bonk* etc. *Literary coinages* have been produced by scholars and literary celebrities; for example, *blatant* (Edmund Spenser, 1590–6), *boojum* and *chortle* (Lewis Carroll, the latter from a blend of *chuckle* + *snort*), *yahoo* (Jonathan Swift, an imaginary race of brutes in *Gulliver's Travels*). Also, personal names, brand names, place names and acronyms are common sources for neologisms, for example *volt* (< Alessandro Volta, Italian scientist and physician, 1745–1827), *sandwich* (< John Montagu, the fourth Lord of Sandwich, 1718–92, an inveterate gambler who chose to eat cold cuts of meat between slices of bread rather than leave the gaming table), *canary* (< Canary Islands), *sherry* (< Jerez, Spain), *denim* (< *serge de Nîmes*, a woolen fabric from Nîmes, France), *calico* (< Calcutta), *pomegranate* (< *pomme de Granada* 'apple of Granada'), *kleenex* (< *Kleenex* brand tissue), *xerox* (< *Xerox*), *Gestapo* (< *Geheime Staatspolizei* 'State Secret Police'), *radar* (< radio direction and ranging) (Campbell 2004: 272–8).

neutralization   Loss or suppression of an opposition between linguistic units. Most typically, loss or suppression in some context of an opposition between phonemes that maintain their contrastive nature in other environments, such as, for example, when in some language final devoicing neutralizes the contrast between voiced and voiceless obstruents word-finally, but the contrast persists in positions other than at the end of words. Because of the sound change of *flapping*, in American English, the contrast between /t/ and /d/ is neutralized between vowels where the first is stressed, so that both *latter* and *ladder* are pronounced the same, with a flapped 'd' in the middle.

new-dialect formation   Process in which, in a mixture of different input **dialects**, it is hypothesized that different variants are leveled out and a single, new, focused dialect arises that is different in some ways from all the input **varieties**. Associated with Peter Trudgill (1986). See also **dialect geography**.

Niger-Congo   A large **language family** of sub-Saharan Africa, to which the very large **Bantu** subfamily belongs. In an extended sense, Niger-Congo is also often used to mean Greenberg's (1963) **Niger-Kordofanian** classification, sometimes adjusted to avoid certain of the problems with some of the 'Kordofanian' groups.

Niger-Kordofanian (now often just called **Niger-Congo**)   A hypothesis of **distant genetic relationship** proposed by Joseph H. Greenberg (1963) in his classification of African languages. Estimated counts of Niger-Kordofanian languages vary from around 900 to 1,500 languages. Greenberg grouped 'West Sudanic' and **Bantu** into a single large family, which he called **Niger-Congo**, after the two major rivers, the Niger and the Congo 'in whose basins these languages predominate' (Greenberg 1963: 7). This included the subfamilies already recognized earlier: (1) West Atlantic (to which Greenberg

joined Fulani, in a Serer-Wolof-Fulani [Fulfulde] group),
(2) Mande (Mandingo) (thirty-five to forty languages),
(3) Gur (or Voltaic), (4) Kwa (with Togo Remnant) and
(5) Benue-Congo (Benue-Cross), with the addition of
(6) Adamawa-Eastern, which had not previously been
classified with these languages and whose classification
remains controversial. For Greenberg, **Bantu** was but
a subgroup of Benue-Congo, not a separate subfamily
on its own. In 1963 he joined **Niger-Congo** and the
'Kordofanian' languages into a larger postulated
phylum, which he called Niger-Kordofanian.

Niger-Kordofanian has numerous supporters but is
not well established; the classification of several of
the language groups Greenberg assigned to Niger-
Kordofanian is rejected or revised, though most scholars
accept some form of Niger-Congo as a valid grouping.
As Nurse (1997: 368) points out, it is on the basis of
general similarities and the noun-class system that
most scholars have accepted Niger-Congo, but 'the fact
remains that no one has yet attempted a rigorous demon-
stration of the genetic unity of Niger-Congo by means of
the Comparative Method.'

Niger-Saharan   see **Congo-Saharan**

Nilo-Saharan   One of Greenberg's (1963) four large **phyla**
in his classification of African languages. In dismantling
the inaccurate and racially biased 'Hamitic,' of which
Nilo-Hamitic was held to be part, Greenberg demonstrated the inadequacy of those former classifications
and argued for the connection between Nilotic and
Eastern Sudanic. He noted that 'the Nilotic languages
seem to be predominantly isolating, tend to mono-
syllabism, and employ tonal distinctions' (Greenberg
1963: 92). To the extent that this classification is based

on commonplace shared typology and perhaps areally diffused traits, it does not have a firm foundation. Nilo-Saharan is disputed, and many are not convinced of the proposed genetic relationships. It is generally seen as Greenberg's wastebasket phylum, into which he placed all the otherwise unaffiliated languages of Africa.

Nilotic   A **language family** of Africa, made of some thirty to fifty **languages** (depending on differing opinions). Most classifications place the Nilotic family or subfamily within the Eastern Sudanic branch of Greenberg's proposed **Nilo-Saharan phylum**.

Nivkh (also called **Gilyak**)   A language **isolate** spoken in the northern part of Sakhalin Island and along the Amur River of Manchuria, in China. There have been various unsuccessful attempts to link Nivkh genetically with various other language groupings, including **Eurasiatic** and **Nostratic**.

non-reciprocal intelligibility (also called **partial intelligibility** and unidirectional intelligibility)   The situation in which speakers of one 'language' understand those of another language, but speakers of that other language do not understand speakers of the first (as is usual with Spanish and Portuguese, as Portuguese speakers often understand Spanish while Spanish speakers typically do not understand Portuguese well). See also **mutual intelligibility**.

Northeast Caucasian   see **Nakh-Dagestan**

Northern Cities Shift   A **vowel shift** (series of innovations in the vowels) in the English spoken in the urban centers that surround the American side of the Great Lakes: Syracuse, Rochester, Buffalo, Cleveland, Toledo, Detroit, Flint, Gary, Chicago and Rockford. The shift begins with (1) /æ/, of *cad*, which moves to the position of the last vowel of idea /ɪ°/; (2) in the shift, the vowel /o/, of *cod*, then shifts so it sounds like *cad*; (3) /oh/ *cawed* moves to the vowel of *cod*; (4) /e/ in *Ked* moves to the vowel of *cud*; (5) the vowel of *cud* moves to *cawed*; and (6) the /ɪ/ in *kid* moves to /e/ of *Ked*. See **chain shift**.

Northwest Caucasian   Also called **Abkhaz-Adyge**

Northwest Coast linguistic area   A **linguistic area** of extensive linguistic diversity extending from northern California to Alaska and including the following **languages** and **language families**: Tlingit, Eyak, several **Athabaskan** languages, Haida, **Tsimshian**, **Wakashan**, **Chimakuan**, **Salishan**, Alsea, Coosan, Kalapuyan, Takelma and Lower Chinook. The area is known for extremely complex phonological systems, with few vowels but many consonants, including series such as, glottalized stops, affricates, fricatives and sometimes nasals, along with labiovelars, multiple laterals (*l*, *ł*, *λ*, *λ'*) and a uvular–velar (*k*, *q*) contrast. Labial consonants are scarce in the region, completely lacking in Tlingit and Tillamook and quite limited in Eyak and Athabaskan. By way of contrast, the uvulars are particularly well represented. Vowel systems tend to be simple, usually with a three- or four-way contrast (*i*, *a*, *u/o*). Pharyngeal consonants occur in several languages. Shared morphological traits include: extensive suffixing, with virtually no prefixes; reduplication (signaling various grammatical functions such as, iteration, continuative, progressive, plural, collective, diminutive etc.); numeral classifiers; alienable/inalienable possession; pronominal plural; nominal plural (optional distributive plural); tense–aspect suffixes; masculine/feminine gender in demonstratives and articles; visible/invisible distinction in demonstratives; aspect (including a momentaneous/durative dichotomy) more important than tense. All but Tlingit have passive-like constructions. The negative is in initial position regardless of the usual word order. Northwest Coast languages also have lexically paired singular and plural verb stems (that is, a lexical root may be required with a plural subject that is entirely different from the root used with a singular subject).

The following traits are shared by a smaller number of languages: (1) a shift of *k > č in Wakashan, Salishan, Chimukuan and some other languages; (2) tone (or pitch-accent contrasts) in Tlingit, Haida, Bella Bella, Upriver Halkomelem, Quileute, Kalapuyan and Takelma; (3) ergative (distinctive marking for agent as opposed to shared marking for intransitive subject and transitive object) in Tlingit, Haida, Tsimishian, some Salishan languages, Sahaptin, Chinookan and Coosan; (4) 'lexical suffixes' (in Wakashan and Salishan) designating familiar objects (ordinarily signaled by independent roots in other languages), for example, body parts, geographical features, cultural artifacts, and some abstract notions. Wakashan, for example, has 300 such suffixes; (5) weakly-developed distinction between nouns and verbs; (6) a sub-area lacking nasals: Twana, Lushootseed (Salishan), Quileute (Chimukuan), Nitinat, Makah (Nootkan branch of Wakashan). The latter two show the following shifts under areal pressure: *m' > b', *n > d and *n' > d'. Other Nootkan languages lack these shifts. See also **areal linguistics**.

Nostratic (< Latin *nostra* 'our')   A proposed **distant genetic relationship** that, as formulated in the 1960s by Illich-

Svitych, would group **Indo-European, Uralic, Altaic, Kartvelian, Dravidian** and **Hamito-Semitic** (later **Afroasiatic**), though other versions of the hypothesis would include various other languages (see Kaiser and Shevoroshkin 1988). Nostratic has a number of supporters, mostly associated with the Moscow school of Nostratic, though a majority of **historical linguists** do not accept the claims.

There are many problems with the evidence presented on behalf of the Nostratic hypothesis. In several instances the proposed reconstructions do not comply with typological expectations; numerous proposed cognates are lax in semantic associations, involve onomatopoeia, are forms too short to deny chance, include nursery forms and do not follow the sound correspondences formulated by supporters of Nostratic. A large number of the putative cognate sets are considered problematic or doubtful even by its adherents. More than one-third of the sets are represented in only two of the putative Nostratic branches, though by its founder's criteria, acceptable cases need to appear in at least three of the Nostratic language families. Numerous sets appear to involve borrowing. (See Campbell 1998, 1999.) It is for reasons of this sort that most historical linguists reject Nostratic.

nursery word, nursery formation (also occasionally called **babbling words**, *mama–papa* **vocabulary**, and, in German, *Lallwörter*) Words of the *mama-nana-papa-dada-caca* sort, sometimes thought to be among children's first words but in fact more typically coined by adults to imitate children's utterances or to address small children. It is generally believed that such words should be avoided in considerations of potential linguistic affinities, since these typically share a high degree of cross-linguistic similarity that is not due to common ancestry.

obsolescence (of languages)   see **endangered languages, language death**

obsolescence (of vocabulary)   The process of a vocabulary item becoming archaic, fading and sometimes disappearing altogether from a **language**, or being otherwise eventually displaced by newer **coinages** or **borrowings**. This process is usually the responce to cultural changes by which the common practices and associated lexicon of one era fall into disuse or are replaced by those of a later one; this has occurred to many of the vocabulary items intimately associated with medieval European institutions and technologies: *catapults, chivalry, feudalism, falconry, flying buttresses, usury, trials by ordeal* etc. (Campbell 2004: 279.) See **lexical change**.

O

o-grade   see **ablaut**

Omotic   A large **language family** of east Africa consisting of some thirty **languages**, mostly in Ethiopia. Omotic was formerly considered a branch of **Cushitic** but as information on the languages became better known this was revised. Some of the Omotic languages are: Dizi, Ometo, Gonga, Aari, Dime. Most now consider Omotic a separate branch of **Afroasiatic**, a generally but not universally accepted **distant genetic relationship**.

onomatopoeia   Property of words that sound like the noise associated with their referent, for example, *bow wow, cuckoo, peep, swish* etc.). Languages may approximate each other in their onomatopoetic words, but rarely agree exactly on how to imitate a barking dog, the wind in the trees and so on. Onomatopoeitic words are sometimes looked upon with suspicion since they violate the general arbitrary relationship between sound and meaning in words. A rule of thumb in attempts to establish genetic relationships among languages is that onomatopoetic forms should be eliminated, since onomatopoetic words from different languages may sound similar to one another because they are imitating sounds in nature, not because they have inherited the similarity from an earlier common ancestor. See also **sound symbolism**.

Otomanguean (also sometimes spelled **Oto-Manguean**)   A large and old **language family** of Mesoamerica, stretching from northern Mexico to Nicaragua. Some members of Otomanguean are Otomí, Pame, Chichimeco, Mazahua, Chinantecan, Popolocan, Zapotecan, Amuzgo and Mixtecan.

overt prestige   The positive or high value attributed to **variables**, **varieties** and **languages**; value judgments typically recognized widely among the speakers of a language. The prestige varieties and variables are usually those recognized as belonging to the standard language or that used by highly educated or influential people. See also **covert prestige, prestige**.

P

Paezan   A **small language** family of Colombia and Ecuador whose membership is not clear; in addition to Paez, it may also contain Andaquí, Coconuco and perhaps a few others. Numerous proposals attempt to link Paezan with other families in larger distant genetic groupings, none of which is estabalished, for example *Paezan-Barbacoan*, *Chibchan-Paezan*, *Macro-Paezan* (with Warao, Itonama, Paezan-Barbacoan, Cunsa-Capishaná) etc.

palatalization   Any **sound change** (also a synchronic phonological process) that makes a sound more palatal, that is, moves the blade of the tongue closer to the hard palate, typically the effect that front vowels and palatal glides have on consonants. In palatalization the body of the tongue is raised toward the hard palate during the articulation of the consonant.

Three types of palatalization occur. One consists of the change of the position of articulation of a consonant from another position (typically *dental, alveolar* or *velar*) to a contact on the palate. In a second type, a palatal glide (offglide) /j/ is taken on as a secondary feature by a non-palatal consonant. Finally, in a third type, palatalization can be seen as a process of **dissimilation** in which a non-palatal consonant acquires a palatal effect in the environment of a *low back* vowel, typically /a/ (e.g. Kiliwa (Yuman) *ča?* [čᵛa?] 'bite'). Examples of the first and second type abound in the synchronic and diachronic phonologies of the world. The third type is rare. In the first type, /t, k/ can become [č] in the environment of a /i/ or /j/: Brazilian Portuguese raises word-final /e, o/ to [i, u], respectively; a /d/ or /t/ preceding such an [i] are palatalized to [ǰ] and [č], respectively: *Rio de Janeiro* [híujižãné(j)ru], *universidade* 'university' [ūnĩversidáʤi], *vinte* 'twenty' [vĩñči], *iate* 'yacht' [jáči]. Palatal assimilation can be progressive, as in Shoshone (Numic branch, Uto-Aztecan) *kuittsu* 'cattle, bison' is [kúču]; in the environment of a preceeding /i/, a Shoshone /n/ is reduced to a nasalized palatal glide [j̃]: *wihnu* 'then' [wĩhj̃ũ ~ wĩhñũ]. Compare non-palatalizing *kettsi'ah* 'to bite' [kitsi'ah], *siimmo-kottsih* 'bladder' [sī:mõɣotsi], *heheppittsionnee(n)* 'old ladies' [hɨhɨpičõnɨɨ] (a palatal affricate but a non-palatal /nn/ [n]). In the second pattern, a consonant acquires a palatal secondary feature; such assimilation can be progressive as well; in Kiliwa (Yuman), the verb *piʔhiw* 'to fly' is [piʔhʸúw]. Examples of regressive assimilation are found in eastern Finnish dialects: *susi > susʸi > susʸ* 'wolf', *tuli > tulʸi > tulʸ* 'fire'. Finally, in the third pattern, we see a dissimilatory palatalization in the word-initial pre-French **k*: **kattu ~ *gattu* 'cat' > *kátus > kátu > kjátu > šá (chat)*, **karu* 'dear' > *kjáru > kjɛrə > šɛr(ə) (cher, chère)*, **kastel* 'castle' > *kató > kjató > šató (château)*, **kan* 'dog' > *kán > kjén > kjẽn > šjɛn ~ šjẽ (chien[ne])*.

'Paleosiberian' languages (also sometimes called **Paleoasiatic**, **Hyperborean languages**)   A geographical (not genetic) designation for several otherwise unaffiliated languages (**isolates**) and small **language families** of Siberia. Perhaps the main thing that unites these languages is that they are not Turkic, Russian or Tungusic, the better known languages of Siberia. Languages often listed as Paleosiberian are: Chukchi, Koryak, Kamchadal (Itelmen), Yukaghir, Yeniseian (Ket) and Nivkh (Gilyak). These have no known genetic relationship to one other.

Pama-Nyungan   A very large, widely spread **language family** of Australia, some 175 **languages**. The name comes from Kenneth Hale, based on the words *pama* 'man' in the far northeast and *nyunga* 'man' in the southwest. Languages assigned to Pama-Nyungan extend over four-fifths of Australia, most of the continent except northern areas. Pama-Nyungan is accepted by most Australianists as a legitimate language family, but not uncritically and not universally. It is rejected by Dixon (2002); it is held by others to be plausible but inconclusive based on current evidence. Some Pama-Nyungan languages are Lardil, Kayardilt, Yukulta, Yidiny, Dyirbal, Pitta-Pitta, Arrente, Warlpiri, Western Desert language(s), and there are many more.

'Papuan' languages   A term of convenience used to refer to the **languages** of the western Pacific, most in New Guinea (Papua New Guinea and the Indonesian provinces of Papua and West Irian Jaya), that are neither **Austronesian** nor **Australian**. Papuan definitely does not refer to a **genetic relationship** among these languages for no such relationship can at present be shown. That is, the term is defined negatively and does not imply a linguistic relationship. While most are spoken on the island of New Guinea, some are found in the Bismark Archipelago, Bougainville Island and the Solomon Islands to the east, and in Halmahera, Timor and the Alor Archipelago to the west. There are some 800 Papuan languages divided in the a large number of mostly small **language families** and **isolates** not demonstrably related to one another. One large genetic grouping that has been posited for a number of Papuan languages is the *Trans-New Guinea phylum*, which is promising but not yet confirmed. Greenberg's **Indo-Pacific** hypothesis of a grand **macro-family** involving Papuan and other languages has mostly been abandoned.

paradigm leveling   see **analogical leveling**

paragoge (from Greek *paragōgé* 'a leading past')   A **sound change** that adds a sound (usually a vowel) to the end of a word. For example, dialects of Spanish sometimes add a final *-e* (sporadically) to some words that end in *-d*: *huéspede* < *huésped* 'guest'; *rede* < *red* 'net'. Several American Indian languages add final vowels to loanwords from Spanish ending in a consonant, for example. Hopi shows such vowels in: *alasáni* < *alazán* 'sorrel (horse)'; *melóni* < *melón* 'melon', *votóóna* < *botón* 'button', *asapráni* < *azafrán* 'saffron', *lestóóni* < *listón* 'ribbon'. Zuni adds final vowels in: *liyá:li* < *real* 'one bit, one eighth of a peso', *wá:kaši* < *vaca(s)* 'cattle'. New Mexico Tewa has *bí:hera* <*virgen* 'virgin'. Examples in Acoma are: *wééyisí* <*bueyes* 'oxen', *merúúni* < *melón* 'melon', *pinsibáári* < *principal* 'village officer'.

parallel innovation (also sometimes called **independent parallel innovation**)   Changes in different **languages** that appear similar but that took place independently of one another. It is important to attempt to distinguish parallel innovations since, for example, they could seem to be **shared innovations** and therefore evidence for **subgrouping** or, in some cases, reasons for classifying languages together in **distant genetic relationships** though, in fact, they are not evidence of closer linguistic kinship.

parent language   see **proto-language**

partial intelligibility   see **mutual intelligibilty, unidirectional intelligibility**

pathway of change   The typical direction of a change seen to recur across languages (for example, the change that voices intervocalic obstruents), or, the typical sequences of intermediate stages a change passes through to get to its final form, for example *s* > *h* > Ø in a number of languages (rather than directly *s* > Ø). Pathways of change in **grammaticalization** refer to recurring grammaticalization changes seen in various languages – for example, that forms meaning 'come', 'go' and 'have' are frequently seen to grammaticalize as future markers. See also **trajectory, directionality**.

pejoration   see **degeneration**

Penutian   A very large proposed **distant genetic relationship** in western North America, suggested originally by Dixon and Kroeber (1913a, 1913b, 1919) for the Californian **language families Wintuan, Maiduan, Yokutsan** and *Miwok-Costanoan*. The name is based on words for 'two', something like *pen* in Wintuan, Maiduan, and Yokutsan, and *uti* in Miwok-Costanoan, joined to form *Penutian*. Sapir (1929), impressed with the hypothesis, attempted to add an Oregon Penutian (Takelma, Coos, Siuslaw, 'Yakonan'), Chinook, Tsimshian, a Plateau Penutian (Sahaptian, 'Molala-Cayuse,' Klamath-Modoc) and a Mexican Penutian (Mixe-Zoquean, Huave).

The Penutian grouping has been influential, and later proposals have attempted to unite various languages from Alaska to Bolivia with it. Nevertheless, it had a shaky foundation based on extremely limited evidence, and, in spite of extensive later research, it did not prove possible to demonstrate any version of the Penutian hypothesis and several prominent Penutian specialists abandoned it. Today it remains controversial and unconfirmed, with some supporters but with many who doubt it. (See Campbell 1997: 309–20.)

philology (< Greek *philologia* 'love of words')   Has several senses. Sometimes philology means the study of some classical or older language – English philology, Germanic philology, **Romance** philology etc. In another sense, philology means **historical linguistics** as practiced in the nineteenth century; what today is called historical linguistics was often referred to earlier as 'philology', as in '**Indo-European** philology'. In yet another sense, philology is the field that attempts to retrieve systematic information about a **language** from written records, for example, to obtain historical information from documents in order to learn about the culture and history of the people behind the text, and, to interpret older written attestations with the goal of obtaining information about the history of the language (or languages) in which the documents are written. This concern with what linguistic information can be acquired from written documents, with how we can get it and with what we can make of the information once we have it, is the sense of philology most common today in historical linguistics. The philological investigation of older written attestations can contribute in several ways – for example, by documenting **sound changes**, distinguishing inherited from borrowed material, dating changes and **borrowings** and helping to understand the development and change in writing systems and orthographic conventions. Results of these studies can have implications for claims about scribal practice, **subgrouping** classification, causes of changes, the **reconstruction** of a **proto-language**, borrowed changes and rules, the identification of **extinct languages** and the historical interpretation of many changes within the languages investigated in this way. Philological investigation of extant written materials is often the only avenue available for the study of extinct native languages or earlier stages of the surviving indigenous languages in several areas of the world.

phonemic conditioning (of sound change)   see **sound change**

phonetic change   see **sound change**

phonetic erosion   see **erosion, grammaticalization**

phonetic interference   Process by which foreign sounds in **loanwords** are changed to conform to native sounds and the permitted phonetic patterns of the **borrowing (recipient)** language. See also **naturalization**.

phonological change   see **sound change**

phonological reconstruction   see **comparative method, reconstruction**

phonologization   see **primary spit, secondary split**

Phrygian   An **Indo-European** language spoken by people who entered Anatolia about 1200 BC and took control. Phrygian inscriptions date to the period from the eighth century BC to the third century AD; by the sixth century AD Phrygian was **extinct**.

phyla   see **phylum**

phylogenetic relationship   A term associated with biology but sometimes applied in linguistics to refer to a **genetic relationship** or **language-family** relationship.

phylum   A proposed **genetic relationship** that would group together **language families** (also isolates) in a larger-scale classification. Potentially, a phylum could refer to a more remote, larger-scale grouping of **languages** where the languages included are in fact confirmed to be related to one another; however, this is seldom the case. More typically, phylum refers to a grouping of languages thought by some to be distantly related to one another, though on the basis of inconclusive evidence, more or less equivalent to **macro-family**. See also **distant genetic relationship**.

pidgin (sometimes called **contact language**) A simplified form of **language**, typically with a reduced grammar and vocabulary, used for communication between groups speaking different languages who have no other language in common, usually in situations where there are strikingly different levels of power in a colonial setting. A pidgin is not spoken as a first or native language.

The process by which pidgins arise is referred to as **pidginization**. As a pidgin becomes the first language of a generation of children, it acquires all the characteristics of a natural language, including a richer vocabulary and a functioning, relatively stable phonology and grammar, and in this way becomes a **creole**. The formation of a **creole** is referred to as **creolization**.

PIE   see **proto-Indo-European**

polygenesis   The hypothesis that human **language** had not a single origin, as in the **monogenesis** theory, but that the breakthrough to human language took place independently more than once, in different places or times. In another sense, polygenesis is applied to a particular language that may be thought to have more than one parent.

Polygenesis also characterizes the now dominant view of the origins of **pidgins** and **creoles** that they do not stem from a single original pidgin language, as in the monogenesis view of pidgin and creole origins.

Pomoan   A **family** of **languages** in northern California several of which are extinct, all of which are endangered. Pomoan languages include (1) Northern Pomo, Central Pomo, Southern Pomo, Kashaya (Southwestern Pomo), Northeastern Pomo, Eastern Pomo and Southeastern Pomo. Pomoan is often associated with the disputed **Hokan** hypothesis of **distant genetic relationship**.

post-creole continuum   see **decreolization**

pre-language   A **reconstruction** of a stage of a language employing structures from later stage(s) of the same language, particularly in **internal reconstruction;** this reconstruction is referred to by the prefix *pre-*, as for example *Pre-English*. This contrasts with a reconstruction arrived at by the **comparative method** (involving multiple languages), for which the prefix *proto-* is employed.

prestige   In **sociolinguistics**, the positive value judgment or high status accorded certain **languages**, certain **varieties** and certain **variables** favored over other less prestigious languages, varieties or variables. The prestige accorded linguistic variables is a factor that often leads to linguistic change. The prestige of a language can lead speakers of other languages to take **loanwords** from it or to adopt the language outright in **language shift. Overt prestige** is the most common; it is the positive or high value attributed to variables, varieties and languages typically widely recognized as prestigious among the speakers of a language. The prestige varieties and variables are usually those recognized as belonging to the standard language or that are used by highly educated or influential people. **Covert prestige** refers to the positive evaluation given to non-standard, low-status or 'incorrect' forms of speech by some speakers, a hidden or unacknowledged prestige for non-standard **variables** that leads speakers to continue using them and sometimes causes such forms to spread to other speakers.

primary split   **Sound change** (sometimes called **conditioned merger**) in which some variant (allophone) of a phoneme ceases to be a member of that original phoneme and in the change becomes a member of some other phoneme instead, leaving a gap in the environments in the language where that orginal phoneme can occur. That is, the phoneme could originally occur in certain contexts in which after the change it is no longer found. In primary split, a variant of a phoneme (an allophone) merges with some other already existing phoneme, but only in certain specific environments and not in others. The total number of phonemes in the language remains the same. **Rhotacism** in Latin illustrates primary split, where intervocalic *s* changes to *r* as seen in English loans from Latin such as *rural* (<*rūs -al*, by rhotacism) but not in *rustic* (Latin *rūs -ticus*, with no rhotacism, since the *s* of *rūs* – 'country, countryside' is not intervocalic); also seen in: *opus*/*opera* (Latin *opus* 'work'), *onus*/*onerous* (Latin *onus* 'burden'), *corpus*/*corpora*/*corporal*/*corporeal* (Latin *corpus* 'body') etc. Since Latin already had *r* as a distinct phoneme, and since only some instances of *s* (just intervocalic ones) shifted to *r*, joining the already existing phoneme *r*, this is an instance of primary split. See also **split, secondary split.**

Primitive   An earlier equivalent of 'Proto-', or 'Common', as in *Primitive Germanic* or *Proto-Germanic*. See **proto-language**.

productive Said of linguistic elements that can be utilized in new circumstances – usually said of morphemes, words or constructions that can combine freely with others to create new occurrences in a language. For example, the suffix *-ness* is very productive in English where it is frequently used to derive new nouns from adjectives, as in, for example, *distinctness, acuteness, sedateness* etc.; it can be attached to verbs to create new words. On the other hand, the suffix *-th* as in *width, length, warmth* is **unproductive** since new nouns are not being created by adding it to adjectives.

productivity see **productive**

progressive assimilation **Sound change** in which an **assimilation** (one sound becoming more similar to another through the influence of a neighboring sound) changes a sound that comes later in the word than (or closer to the right end of the word than) the sound that conditions the change. For example, in the change from **Proto-Indo-European** *kolnis > Latin *collis* 'hill', the *n* that undergoes the change is after (to the right of) the *l* that conditions the change. See **assimilation**.

proportional analogy The type of **analogy** that can be described by the equation a : b = b : x in which one solves for 'x' – *a* is to *b* as *b* is to *what?* An example is *ride: rode* = *dive : x*; thus, an original English past tense form *dived* was replaced by *dove* (in many dialects), under pressure from *drive : drove, write : wrote, strive : strove* etc. Both *dived* and *dove* are considered to be correct. See **analogical leveling**.

prothesis (< Greek *pro-* 'before', *thesis* 'placing') **Sound change** in which a sound, usually a vowel, is added or inserted at the beginning of words. Sometimes considered to be a type of word-initial **epenthesis**, the most frequent motivation for such a process is the elimination of a word-initial consonant cluster by adding the vowel that re-syllabifies the word. In western Romance, a rule inserting an *e* or *i* yielded the following examples: Latin *skola* 'school' > Vulgar Latin *iskola* > Spanish *escuela*, Portuguese *escola* [iškɔlə], French *école*; Latin *skūtu* 'shield' > Vulgar Latin *iskudu* > Spanish *escudo* [eskúðo], Portuguese *escudo* [iškúdu ~ iškúðu], French *écu*. Compare the following examples from Nahuatl **kši* 'foot' > *ikši*; cf. *no-kši* 'my foot'. See also **insertion**.

Proto-Indo-European (in former times sometimes called **Indo-Germanic** after the German version **Indo-Germanisch**) The parent **language** from which the languages of the **Indo-European** language family descend – presumed to have once been an actual spoken language – also the results of attempts to reconstruct this language by means of the **comparative method**. Most of the tenets of the comparative method and the techniques of **linguistic reconstruction** were developed in work aimed at recovering Proto-Indo-European and some of its subfamilies, Germanic and Romance in particular. Often abbreviated as **PIE**.

proto-language (also sometimes **proto language**, **proto-language**) The once-spoken ancestral language from which **daughter languages** descend, and, in another sense, the language reconstructed by the **comparative method** that represents the ancestral language from which the compared languages descend. To the extent that the **reconstruction** by the comparative method is accurate, the once actually spoken proto-language and the proto-language as reconstructed by the comparative linguist should coincide. Also sometimes called **common, primitive**. See, for example, **Proto-Indo-European**.

Proto-World (also sometimes called **Proto-Human, Proto-Sapiens**, the **Mother Tongue**, 'proto-language' and the **roots of language**) 'Conjectural protolanguage from which, according to some applications of mass comparison, all later languages have developed' (Matthews 1997: 302). See also **global etymology**. (Bengtson and Ruhlen 1994a, 1994b.) See also **monogenesis**.

pull chain (also called **drag chain**) A **chain shift** in which one change may create a hole in the phonemic pattern (an asymmetry, a gap) that is followed by another change that fills the hole by 'pulling' in some other sound from the system, and, if the sound that shifted to fill the original hole in the pattern leaves a new hole of its own elsewhere in the pattern, then another change may 'pull' some other sound in to fill that gap in a chain of inter-related changes. For example, in **Grimm's Law**, the voiceless stops (p, t, k) first changed to fricatives (f, θ, h) leaving a gap for the voiceless stops, then that gap was filled by the change of voiced stops (b, d, g) > voiceless stops (p, t, k), which in turn left a gap filled by the last part of Grimm's Law in which voiced aspirates (bh, dh, gh) > plain voiced stops (b, d, g) filling the gap of the missing voiced stops. See also **push chain**.

punctuated equilibrium model An approach to language prehistory advocated by R. M. W. Dixon (1997); he believes that there were long periods of equilibrium during which languages coexisted in relative harmony in a given region without any major changes taking place, but that sometimes the state of equilibrium was punctuated by some cataclysmic event causing sweeping changes in the linguistic situation and possibly triggering languages to split up and expand, 'appropriately modelled by a family tree diagram'.

> The punctuation could be due to some natural event (floods, drought, volcanic eruption), or to the emergence of an aggressive political or religious group, or to some striking technical innovation, or simply to entry into new and pristine territory. After the events which caused the punctuation have run their course, a new state of equilibrium will come into being.' (Dixon 1997: 67; see also Dixon 2002: 32–5.)

There are, however, problems with this idea. Dixon's correlation of states of equilibrium with extensive contact-induced diffusion and punctuation events with diversification into **language families** is linguistically unrealistic and has several difficulties.

The notion of punctuated equilibrium is challenged in biology – evolution continues even without punctuated events disrupting equilibrium. Language change and differentiation into language families also continue in periods of equilibrium (in the absence of disruptive events). Another problem has to do with the unrealistic assumptions about social structure and its relation to linguistic change. The ethnographic literature does not support a picture of small-scale traditional or non-industrial societies as living egalitarian and harmonious lives, as Dixon sees it. Rather, it shows enormous variation in social structure and political organization in which harmony and equality are mostly absent. However, since Dixon's model of punctuated equilibrium in language change crucially depends on this view of society, this constitutes a serious problem for the approach.

Dixon equates equilibrium with convergence. Nevertheless, normal change leading to diversification into language families can and does take place in situations of equilibrium, contrary to expectations of the model. We see numerous cases in which, under stable conditions over long periods of time, with no evidence of punctuation, the languages of the region continue to undergo normal change and to diversify into language families. A significant number of language families appear to have developed *in situ*, in relative harmony and without punctuation events, as Dixon (1997: 9–70) also acknowledges. Another problem comes from the situations of equilibrium without diffusion, contrary to the expectations of the model. Dixon (1997: 70–1) believes that in periods of equilibrium 'languages in contact will diffuse features between each other, becoming more and more similar. These similarities will gradually converge'. But, linguistic diffusion does not always take place in situations of harmonious equilibrium. Languages in the same area over a long time may exhibit little evidence of contact-induced change, for example, **Athabaskans** of the American Southwest (Navajo, Apache) and their non-Athabaskan neighbors (Hopi, Zuni, Keresan and Tanoan groups). The Hano Tewa (Tanoan language) and Hopi (Uto-Aztecan) harmoniously share the same tiny mesa top, yet extremely little borrowing or diffusion has taken place in either language. This is a problem for the model's expectation that equilibrium gives diffusion and convergence. Punctuation situations, for Dixon, are correlated with changes leading to diversification, not with diffusion. However, contrary to this expectation, linguistic diffusion can be caused by punctuation events and does not take place just in equilibrium. Conquest and political inequality are great promoters of structural diffusion among languages, and examples are so common as scarcely to bear comment. For example, the history of English is mostly that of punctuation, with the strong impact on the language from Scandinavia through the Scandinavian invasion and from French due to the Norman conquest, but the outcome is more in tune with that envisaged for equilibrium states: English assimilated huge amounts of vocabulary, borrowed sounds and some pronouns and leveled morphosyntactic complexity. Both forced language contact (punctuation) and peaceful contact (equilibrium) can have similar outcomes with respect to diffusion and convergence.

In short, the correlation envisaged, which equates equilibrium with convergence and punctuation with divergence, is not supported – both kinds of change take place in both kinds of situations. The notion provides no real purchase on the questions of language relationships and of why and how languages diversify. They diversify and spread in both punctuation and equilibrium.

push chain (also called **drag chain**)   A **chain shift** in which the notion is applied that differences between sounds in phonemic systems tend to be maintained to preserve meaning differences of words that otherwise would come to sound alike. In this view, if a sound starts moving into the articulatory space of another sound, this can cause a change in which the crowded sound moves away from the encroaching sound in order to maintain distinctions. If the fleeing sound is pushed towards the articulatory space of some other sound then that sound too may shift to avoid the encroachment, setting of a chain reaction: a push chain.

Q

Quechuan The **language family** to which the various Quechua **languages** belong, spoken by about 8.5 million people in Peru, Bolivia, Ecuador, Argentina and Colombia. The family has two major branches: the one called variously Central Quechua, Quechua I, Quechua B and Huaihuash has such member languages as Huaylas, Conchucos, Huánuco, Yaru etc.; and the one called variously Peripheral Quechua, Quechua II, Quechua A and Huampuy contains Cuzco Quechua, Ayacucho and the various varieties of Ecuador and Argentina among many others. **Varieties** of Quechuan were widely spread by the Inca Empire, associated with the language of its Cuzco capital. Quechuan is not known to have any demonstrable relatives, though a plausible but disputed hypothesis would connect Quechuan and **Aymaran** in the **Quechumaran** hypothesis.

Quechumaran Proposed **distant genetic relationship** that would join **Quechuan** and **Aymaran**. While considerable evidence has been gathered in support of the hypothesis, it is extremely difficult in this case to distinguish what may be inherited (and therefore evidence of a genetic relationship) from what may be diffused (and therefore not reliable evidence of a genetic connection). (Campbell 1995, 1997: 273–83.)

R

raising (opposite of **lowering**) A change in which any sound is seen to rise in terms of its articulation in the mouth; usually it refers to vowel changes in which a vowel becomes higher. For example, in the **Great Vowel Shift** in English former /e:/ and /o:/ were raised to /i:/ and /u:/ respectively, *geese* (formerly /ge:s/, now /gi:s/) and *goose* (/goːs/ > /guːs/) among other associated changes. The opposite of raising is **lowering**.

rate of loss   see **glottochronology**

rate of retention (also **retention rate**)   see **glottochronology**

real-time study   The study of **language change**, typically **sound change**, by comparison of representations of a language (usually of a particular community) recorded or written at different times to detect change that has taken place in the intervals between the earlier and later forms of the language. In sociolinguistic research on change real-time study is often contrasted or opposed to **apparent-time study**. See also **change in progress**.

reality of reconstructions   Linguistic **reconstructions** are hypotheses about the **proto-language**. A good reconstruction may be close to the actual ancestral language once spoken, though a reconstruction may also not approximate that real language very closely in some cases. The success of any given reconstruction depends on the material at hand to work with and the ability of the comparative linguist to figure out what happened in the history of the languages being compared. In cases where the **daughter languages** preserve clear evidence of what the parent language had, a reconstruction can be very successful, matching closely the actual spoken proto-language from which the compared daughters descend. However, there are many cases in which all the daughter languages lose or merge formerly contrasting sounds or eliminate earlier alternations through analogy, or lose words and morphological categories due to changes of various sorts. One cannot recover things about the proto-language via the **comparative method** if the daughters simply do not preserve evidence of them. In cases in which the evidence is severely limited or unclear, linguists often make mistakes. They make the best inferences they can based on the evidence available and on everything known about the nature of human languages and linguistic change. Often the results are very good, sometimes they are less complete. In general, the longer in the past the proto-language split up, the more linguistic changes will have accumulated, and the more difficult it becomes to reconstruct with full success.

In discussions of the reality of reconstructions, some scholars, emphasizing the hypothetical nature of the enterprise, have insisted the reconstructions need have no reality at all, that they merely represent formulas that chart the examples in the compared languages. Most, however, view the reconstructions as genuine attempts to recover real aspects of the parent language, knowing that in most instances this will be at best an approximation of what the proto-language really contained.

A comparison of reconstructed Proto-Romance with attested Latin provides perspective. We do successfully recover a great deal of the formerly spoken language via the comparative method. However, the modern **Romance** languages for the most part preserve little of the former noun cases and complex tense–aspect verbal morphology that Classical Latin had as they descend from Vernacular or Vulgar Latin reconstructed as proto-Romance. Subsequent changes have obscured this inflectional morphology so much that much of it is not reconstructible by the comparative method.

realization   see **actualization**

reanalysis   A change in which the structure of a linguistic element, usually syntactic or morphological, takes on a different analysis from that which it had before the change, that is, a change in which it is assigned a different structure from what it formerly had. Reanalysis is one of only three primary **mechanisms of syntactic change**, **extension** and **syntactic borrowing** being the other two. Reanalysis changes the underlying structure of a syntactic construction, but does not modify the surface manifestation. An axiom of reanalysis is: *Reanalysis depends on the possibility of more than one analysis of a given construction*. For example, in the development of be *going to* from a verb of motion to a 'future' auxiliary the construction came to have two possible interpretations. Originally sentence (a) had just one analysis:

(a) *Laura is going to marry George.*
      Laura is going$_{\text{VERB OF MOTION}}$ to marry George.

But later it came to have a second possible interpretation, as in (b), where *be going (to)* was reanalyzed as a 'future auxiliary':

(b) *Laura is going to marry George.*
      Laura is going$_{\text{FUTURE AUXILIARY}}$ to marry George.

In the reanalysis that produced (b), the future auxiliary, the surface manifestation remained unchanged – (a) and (b) are the same in form, but, are not the same in internal structure or meaning, which changed in the reanalysis. In this case, (a) came to have more than one possible analysis – it underwent reanalysis, yielding (b) with its different structural analysis.

recipient language see **borrowing, donor language, language contact**

reconstruction Postulation of the ancestral form or of earlier stages of a language or elements in a language based on the evidence available. The dominant methods for reconstruction in **historical linguistics** are the **comparative method** and **internal reconstruction**. The comparative method aims at recovering aspects of the **proto-language**, the ancestor from which forms in various **daughter languages** descend; by comparing what the daughter languages inherited from their ancestor, the linguist attempts to reconstruct the linguistic traits that the proto-language possessed. Internal reconstruction aims at arriving at a stage of a given language prior to various conditioned changes the language may have undergone. The success of reconstruction depends upon the extent to which evidence of the original traits is preserved in the languages, upon the knowledge and ability of the linguist in applying the techniques of the comparative method and upon internal reconstruction. See also **lexical reconstruction, phonological reconstruction, morphological reconstruction, syntactic reconstruction, reality of reconstructions.**

recurrent correspondence   see **sound correspondence**

reduced-grade   see **ablaut**

reduction   Language change that results in a decrease in the size or intensity of some linguistic element or in its loss, usually associated with **sound change** or the loss of phonological material or with **erosion** of phonetic material often thought to accompany **grammaticalization.**

reflex   The sound in a **daughter language** that descends from a particular sound of the **proto-language**. The original sound of the proto-language is said to be reflected by the sound which descends from it in a daughter language.

Elements other than just sounds, for example morphemes or grammatical constructions, can also reflect the elements of the proto-language from which they descend.

regressive assimilation (also called **anticipatory assimilation**) **Sound change** in which an **assimilation** (one sound becoming more similar to another through the influence of a neighboring sound) changes a sound that comes earlier in the word than (closer to the beginning of the word than) the sound that conditions the change. For example, in the change Latin *octo* / okto / > Italian *otto* 'eight', the *k* is before the *t* that conditions it to change, a regressive assimilation.

regularity hypothesis (also called the **Neogrammarian hypothesis** and sometimes the **regularity principle**)   The claim of the **Neogrammarians** that **sound change** is regular, or, by their slogan, that 'sound laws suffer no exceptions'. One of the most important basic assumptions in **historical linguistics** is that sound change is regular. To say this means that the change takes place unfailingly whenever the sound or sounds that undergo the change are found in the phonological environments that condition the change. For example, original *p* regularly became *b* between vowels in Spanish (p > b /V __ V); this means that in this context, between vowels, every original *p* became a *b*; it is not the case that some original intervocalic *p*'s became *b* in some words but became, say, *s* in other words and were lost in still others in unpredictable ways.

The Neogrammarian claim for the regularity of sound change has occasionally been challenged, though its fundamental validity has held up well. For example, **dialectologists** with their slogan '**every word has its own** history' opposed the claim, but their examples very often reflected **dialect borrowing**, reaffirming that sound change is regular in its own phonological system. **Lexical diffusion** challenges the claimed classic mechanical regularity of sound change, but most instances of lexical diffusion also turned out to involve dialect borrowing or to be inaccurately analyzed. Claims of **morphological conditioning** of sound change would require modifying the claim of regularity subject only to phonetic conditions, though the notion of morphological conditioning is not supported by all scholars. Otherwise, seeming exceptions to sound changes usually have other explanations, from **analogy, borrowing** etc.

regularity of sound change   see **regularity hypothesis, Neogrammarians**

regularity principal   see **regularity hypothesis**

reinterpretation   While **reanalysis** typically has to do with the reassignment of syntactic or morphemic boundaries (for example, Arabic *naranž* > English *a norange* > *an orange*, with a reanalysis of the *n* as part of the article rather than belonging directly to the article), *reinterpretation* involves a change in syntactic and semantic category; for example, in *that was fun* > *that was a fun game*, the noun *fun* is reinterpreted as the adjective *fun*. See also **mechanisms of syntactic change**.

relative chronology   The apparent order in which linguistic changes took place. A linguistic change takes place at some particular time, and different changes taking place at different times have a temporal order or sequence, some earlier, others later, though usually the exact time of the changes cannot be determined directly. However, based on the linguistic evidence, it is often possible to determine the temporal order (sequence) of the changes without exact dates – their relative chronology. The different stages of **Grimm's Law** illustrate a relative chronology. First, **Proto-Indo-European** *p, *t, *k > f, θ, h in **Germanic**; at a later stage, Proto-Indo-European *b, *d, *g > p, t, k in Germanic. The relative chronology of these two changes is clear, since if the second (voiced stops > voiceless) had taken place before the first (voiceless stops > fricatives), then all stops would have ended up as voiceless fricatives, both the original voiceless stops and the later ones from the change of voiced stops to voiceless. Thus, clearly, the voiceless stops became fricatives first, and then, once these were changed and out of the way, the voiced stops later became voiceless in that relative chronology (order) of the two changes. See also **chronology, absolute chronology**.

relexification   Process of massive lexical replacement associated with **pidgin, creole** or **mixed languages** by which one language imports vocabulary heavily from another, replacing earlier lexical items from the **recipient** language. Relexification can obfuscate **genetic relationships**, as in the case of **Albanian**, which was not originally acknowledged as an **Indo-European** language due to the presence of a large numbers of loans from Turkish and other languages, and as in Armenian, which was thought to belong to the **Iranian** branch of Indo-European until the massive lexical **borrowings** from Iranian were identified. In the **monogenesis** theory of pidgin and creole origins, it is claimed that relexification of an originally Portuguese-based pidgin provided for the development of creoles based on other European languages, French, English etc. See also **loanword**.

relic   see **archaism**

relic area   In **dialect geography,** a region that has remained relatively unaffected by innovations occurring elsewhere within the linguistic territory where other **dialects** or **varieties** of the language are found. See also **focal area, transition area.**

remodeling   see **analogical leveling, rephonologization**

remote relationship, remote linguistic kinship   see **distant genetic relationship**

repertoire of codes (sometimes called **verbal repertoire**) The totality of linguistic **codes** (**lects, varieties, dialects, languages**) regularly employed in the course of socially significant interaction. A typical repertoire of codes in villages of India might include the following: **vernacular** (learned at home), caste dialect, regional standard variety (used in larger towns, on market day, with traveling peddlers), provincial standard variety (learned in school or in the army, in distant cities through pilgrimage etc.), other languages, for example, often Sanskrit and English (learned through formal education, used in business and for religious purposes respectively) and other Indian languages.

rephonemicization   Phonological change that results in a redistribution (reassignment) of phones among the phonemes of a language, as in, in particular, **splits** and **mergers.** See also **rephonologization.**

rephonologization   Jakobson's (1931) term for a change in the phonetic relations among phonemes of a language that does not alter the number of the phonemes.

residual zone   Earlier name for **accretion zone.**

residue   A form or set of forms that do not conform to changes in the language as formulated by the linguist, thus being either exceptions to the change or evidence that the statement of the change or changes needs revision.

restructuring   A change, in generative accounts of linguistic change, that alters the form of the grammar of a language as children acquire a form of grammar whose internal structure (underlying forms, rules) is different from that of the grammar of the generation before them.

retention   Any linguistic material (word, sound, construction) that has not been lost or replaced since the **proto-language** or since some designated earlier period in the history of the language. **Shared retentions** are not considered reliable evidence for **subgrouping,** since sister languages that share retentions need not have had any shared history since the break up of the proto-language (that is, they need not belong to the same subgroup); they need only preserve something they always had. Sometimes **retention** is also used as an equivalent of **archaism, relic.**

retroflexion   **Sound change** in which a sound becomes a retroflex. For example, in the *ruki*-**rule** of Sanskrit, where *s* becomes retroflex after *i, k, r* or *l* unless final or followed by *r*.

retrograde formation   see **back formation**

reversal of language shift   see **endangered languages**

reversal of merger   An axiom is that **mergers are irreversible**. When sounds have completely merged, a later change will not be able to restore the original distinctions. For example, after Sanskrit merged *e, o, a > a,* children learned all words that formerly had *e, o, a* as having only the vowel *a,* and therefore there was no basis for determining which of their words with *a* may have originally had *e* or *o,* or which had retained original *a* unchanged – it was impossible for them to segregate their words with *a* accurately into those that originally had different vowels. Hence, mergers are irreversible.

Occasionally some examples appear to be instances of reversal of merger, but these are not real instances of complete mergers that then reverse, but rather typically involve cases where the merger was not complete in its own variety or where it affected some varieties but not others. An example is the seeming merger towards the end of the nineteenth century of *v* and *w* in some southern England dialects, especially in Cockney, East Anglian and southeastern dialects, with *walley* for *valley, willage* for *village* (and also with **hypercorrection,** *voif* for *wife*). This merger disappeared: it was stigmatized in local speech, and the greater **prestige** of the non-merged pronunciations in more standard dialects – in which the merger had not taken place – won out, making it appear that the merger was reversed, when in fact no such reversal took place. Rather, the merger was simply lost with the adoption of the more prestigious non-merged pronunciation that had always been extant in the speech community.

rhotacism (< Greek *rhotakismos* 'use of *r*, change to *r*') **Sound change** in which a sibilant /s, z/ becomes /r/. (Also the name of the **synchronic** process in which /s, z/ becomes /r/ in a phonological rule.) In **Indo-European,**

Latin and Germanic underwent rhotacism intervocalically, as in Early Latin *honōs-is* > *honōr-is* 'of honor' (genitive case); *honōs* 'honor' (nominative) retained the final -*s* for a long time but then later changed to *honōr* 'honor' by analogy with the other forms of the paradigm, like *honōr-is*, which had *r*. Similarly, **Proto-Germanic** *maizōn* 'greater' rhotacized to become German *mehr* 'more' and English *more*.

Ritwan   see **Algic**

Romance (< Latin *romanice* 'to behave or to speak as a Roman, in the Roman way or manner')   A term referring generically to languages that descended from a form of Latin often referred to as 'Vulgar Latin' (that is, 'vernacular, popular' or 'people's Latin' from *vulgus* '[common] people'), which has also been independently reconstructed using the **comparative method**, to give *Proto-Romance*. The vernacular variety of Latin differs considerably, in all regards (lexicon, phonology, morphology and syntax), from the elite variety known as Classical Latin, which is abundantly attested in the literary texts of Roman antiquity. Ironically, the Classical variety was spoken by a tiny social elite only. The popular variety, on the other hand, was mostly unwritten but spoken by a vast, illiterate majority. That is to say, documentation of Vulgar Latin is limited to certain marginal writings such as wall graffiti, hex shards used by the practitioners of witchcraft, treatises on grammatical and orthographic correctness (for example, the **Appendix Probi**) and technical manuals on agriculture, animal husbandry and veterinary science etc., destined for technical experts of lower social status. Classical authors such as Plautus and Petronius, incorporated stigmatized popular speech in their works.

Romance spread throughout the western Mediterranean as the Roman Empire expanded and eventually developed into the many regional varieties that would later become the 'Romance languages': *Italian, Rumanian, Dalmatian, Sardinian, French, Rhaeto-Romansch, Occitan, Gascon, Ladin (Judeo-Spanish), Catalan, Castilian, Gallego-Portuguese* etc. The differentiation of certain regional **dialects** tended to reflect the relative chronology of conquest of the different provinces of the empire; for example, the Iberian and Balkan forms of Romance, spoken in the earliest regions to be conquered, tended to preserve archaisms later displaced elsewhere by innovations originating in the central regions of the empire (namely, northern Italy and Gaul) that were conquered later (see **relic area**). Several ancient regional dialects became extinct, usually through conquest by speakers of other languages, such as *Berber, Arabic, Germanic* and *Slavic*. See also **dialect geography**.

root creation   A neologism or lexical **coinage** created *ex nihilō*, that is, not out of already existing words in a **language**. Some examples of root creations are: *blurb* (coined by Gelett Burgess, an American humorist, in 1907; *gas* [xas] coined by Dutch chemist, J. B. van Helmont in 1632, inspired by Greek *khaos* [xáos] 'chaos', in which the Dutch letter *g* is pronounced [x] as in the Greek source, a fact lost in other *recipient languages*, such as English, where it is pronounced [g]. See also **neologism**.

rounding   **Sound change** in which a sound takes on lip-rounding; usually, rounding refers to some vowel becoming a round vowel, though it can (more rarely) also apply to consonants that become labialized. See also **labialization**.

***ruki*-rule**   A *sandhi* rule of Sanskrit phonology by which *s* is replaced by *ṣ* after a vowel other than short or long *a* [mostly *i*], or after *k*, *r* or *l*, unless final or followed by *r* (for example, *agni-* 'fire' + *-su* 'locative' > *agniṣu* 'among the fires'). A **sound change** that took place in the phonological environment after *r, *u, *k, *i, *g, *gh (except when a stop followed) – named for the sounds in the environment of the change – in which Proto-Indo-European *s became retroflexed *ṣ* in Indo-Iranian and palatalized *š* in Slavic, in which it later went on to *x*.

rule inversion   A change (and a synchronic process) in which the input and the change are reversed so that the result of the change (or of the rule) is thought to represent the underlying or basic form and the original underlying basic material is thought to be the result of the change or rule. Perhaps the best known example of rule inversion is the treatment of morpheme-final *r* in those **dialects** of English that historically lost this *r* before consonants (*car park* [ka pak]), but maintained it before vowels (*car engine* [kar ɛnǰɪn]), *r* > Ø / __ + C. In dialects with rule inversion, speakers apparently re-analyzed the set of circumstances, believing rather that *r* was inserted before following morphemes that begin in a vowel, Ø > *r* / __ + V, leading to insertion of *r* in cases where, historically, there was no *r*, as in *draw[r]ing* 'drawing' and *law[r] and order* pronounced like 'lore and order'.

rule loss   A language change in which a phonological rule that formerly applied to the language ceases to apply and disappears. For example, the rule that devoiced final obstruents in Yiddish is said to have been lost. Thus Yiddish *bild* 'picture' before the rule loss was [bɪlt] (contrast *Bilder* [bɪld-er] 'pictures', where the *d* remained voiced because it was not in final position); Standard German did not lose the rule and so still has [bɪlt] for *Bild* 'picture' (and *Bilder* with [d], where it is non-final. In Yiddish, however, the rule of final devoicing was completely lost. See **loss**.

S

Salish, Salishan A **language family**, of some twenty-five languages, of the northwest of North America. Some Salishan languages are Bella Coola, Comox, Squamish, Lushootseed, Twana, Quinault, Tillamook, Thompson, Shuswap, Okanagan, Kalispel and Coeur d'Alene.

sandhi In the most general sense, the modification of a sound or of the phonological form of a word under the influence of a preceding or following sound. More specifically, any phonological process that applies to sequences of sounds across a morpheme boundary or across a word boundary. When the change is across a morpheme boundary, it is called *'internal sandhi'*. For example, in Sanskrit a dental stop or nasal after a retroflex consonant [but not after *r*] is replaced by the corresponding retroflex, as in *dviṣ* 'hate' + *-ta-* [perfect passive participle] > *dviṣṭa* 'hated'). When the change takes place across word boundaries, it is called *external sandhi*. For example, in Sanskrit a final *t* before an initial *l* is replaced by *l*, as in *tat* 'that' + *labhate* 'he receives' > *tal labhate* 'he receives that'. The word *Sandhi* comes from the ancient Hindu grammatical tradition, meaning 'union', from *sam* 'together' + *dhi* 'to place'.

satem language Any **Indo-European** language from the **branches** of the family in which velar stops become fricatives or affricates, distinguished from the **centum**

languages, which did not undergo this change. The name reflects Avestan *satəm* 'hundred', since the word for 'hundred' across these languages illustrates the change of the velar stop /k/. Satem languages include those of the **Indo-Iranian** (Indic + Iranian), Armenian, Phrygian, Thracian, Albanian and Balto-Slavic (Baltic + Slavic) branches.

Scythian   see **Scythian hypothesis**

Scythian hypothesis   Early recognition of **Indo-European** as a family of related languages is connected with the 'Scythian hypothesis'. In the writings of the Classical authors (Herodotus, Strabo, Dexippeus, Justin) *Scythica* (from Greek *skuthia*) referred to a nation who inhabited the region to the north of the Black Sea. Some in the eighteenth century equated the Scythians with Tartars, some with Goths and some attributed to them a great empire, later said to be centered in Persia. Josephus and early Christian writers took the Scythians, who by that time had become mythical, to be the descendants of Japheth, son of Noah and assumed father of Europe. These notions were the prelude to later proposed Scythian linguistic identifications. Today, archaeological and linguistic evidence suggests an Iranian identification for the Scythians. The Scythian linguistic hypothesis, which saw several Indo-European languages as **genetically related,** was proposed first by Johannes Goropius Becanus (Jan van Gorp van der Beke) (1569) who emphasized 'Scythian' as the source of several languages, a notion that initiated the recognition of Indo-European as a **language family.** Franciscus Raphelengius (Ravlenghien) reported correspondences between Persian and Germanic languages that he thought showed a genetic affinity. Bonaventura Vulcanius (de Smet) (1597) published several **cognates** among some Indo-European languages, for example such Persian–Dutch comparisons as <berader>/broeder 'brother', <dandan>/tand 'tooth', <dochtar>/dochter 'daughter', <mus>/muis 'mouse', <nam>/naam 'name', <nau>/nieuw 'new', <ses>/zes 'six' and <lab>/lip 'lip' concluding there was a historical affinity between the languages. Various other scholars of the period supported the 'Scythian hypothesis'. Marcus Boxhorn(ius), Claudius Salmasius (Claude de Saumaise), Georg Stiernhielm and Andreas Jäger presented compelling 'Scythian' evidence in the seventeenth century relating Latin, Greek, German, Gothic and Persian, also the Romance, Slavic and Celtic languages, long before Sir William Jones, who is usually given credit for the discovery of Indo-European.

Second Germanic Consonant Shift (also called the **High German Consonant Shift**)   A rather far-reaching **sound change** affecting southern 'High' German dialects, and thus distinguishing them from the northern 'Low' German dialects, which basically turned voiceless stops into affricates word-initially (also after another consonant and when geminated): p > pf, t > ts, k > kx, and into geminate fricatives elsewhere (mostly medially and finally): p > ff, t > ss, k > xx. The change is seen relatively well in Standard High German, though the k > kx is not seen and the geminate fricatives are no longer pronounced as geminates. German *Pfeffer* 'pepper' shows both the p > pf and pp > ff changes; *Zunge* [tsʊŋə] 'tongue' shows t > ts, and *Fuss* 'foot' t > ss; and *Koch* [kox] 'cook' shows k > kx (later to *x*).

secondary split (also called **phonologization** sometimes)   **Sound change** in which allophones of a phoneme cease to be just allophones but become contrastive, adding a new phoneme to the phonological inventory of the language – the total number of phonemes in the language increases. Secondary split can come about only as a consequence of an accompanying **merger** or **loss** (merger with 'zero') of a sound, so that the environment that conditioned the formerly non-contrastive distribution of the sounds (former allophones) changes in such a way that the complementary distribution of the allophones is no longer detectible after the merger that causes the split, but was visible in an earlier stage of the language, before the merger took place. For example, in Old Russian **palatalization** of consonants was conditioned by a following front vowel and was thus predictable (allophonic), as in: *krovĭ* [krovʲɪ] 'blood'; *krovŭ* [krovŭ] 'shelter' with no front vowel lacked the phonetic palatalization. Later, the short/lax final vowels *ĭ* and *ŭ* were lost (merged with Ø ['zero']), leaving /vʲ/ and /v/ in contrast and therefore as distinct phonemes, with new minimal pairs *krovʲ* 'blood' and *krov* 'shelter' due to the merger with Ø (loss) of the final vowels, where the front one had originally conditioned the allophonic palatalization so that the palatalized and non-palatalized variants were merely allophones of a single phoneme. The *v* and *vʲ* split as a result of the merger with Ø where the conditioning front vowel was lost. See also **split**, **primary split**.

semantic attrition   see **semantic bleaching**

semantic bleaching (also sometimes called **desemanticization**, **semantic fading**, **semantic attrition**, **semantic decay**, **semantic depletion**, **semantic impoverishment** and **weakening**)   Loss of conventional semantic content, particularly in **grammaticalization**, when a lexical item loses its lexical semantic content and comes to signal a grammatical marker, as, for example, when *will*, originally meaning 'want', came to mean 'future'.

semantic broadening   see **broadening**

semantic change   Change in meaning. The principal kinds of semantic change, as traditionally classified, are **degeneration (pejoration)**, **elevation (amelioration)**, **hyperbole**, **litotes**, **metaphor**, **metonymy**, **synecdoche**, **narrowing** and **widening**.

semantic displacement   A phenomenon associated with **linguistic acculturation** as a consequence of **language contact** by which a language may come to employ a native term for a newly introduced, foreign referent, thereby necessitating the innovation of a new term for the original native referent. Such a term may be derived in some manner from the original native item, hence the term *semantic displacement*. For example, in Kiliwa, a Yuman language of Baja California (Mexico), pre-contact *xpiip* 'Ephedra', after contact, shifted its meaning to the agricultural referent 'bean(s)' introduced either by Europeans or from pre-contact trade with the horticultural tribes of the nearby Colorado River. The original native referent was then modified by the descriptive relative clause *pi-y-l-t-k^w-yaq* 'that which lies in desolation' (compare *pi* 'die', *pi-y* 'desolate, wilderness'), or more simply 'wild Ephedra'. Other examples of this process of **lexical innovation** in Kiliwa are: *xaq* 'deer' > 'beef', *xaq-piy-l-t-k^w-yaq* (literally 'cattle wilderness'), *?muw* 'mountain sheep (ovis canadiensis)' > 'European sheep', *mx^waa* 'badger; bear' > 'pig', *xma?* 'quail' > 'poultry', *nmi?* wildcat' > '(domestic) cat' (compare *nmi?-?tay* 'cougar, puma'; lit. 'wildcat large'). See also **semantic shift, semantic change**.

semantic fading   see **semantic bleaching**

semantic loan   see **calque, loan translation**

semantic merger   Process that involves the loss of a semantic distinction, typically through the introduction of a term that neutralizes the contrast, as was the case when some **Romance** languages borrowed Germanic *blank* 'white, bare' replacing two separate Latin words with distinct, though related meanings, namely *albus* 'white' and *candidus* 'shining white'.

semantic narrowing   see **narrowing**

semantic shift   see **semantic change**

semantic split   Process in which an item adds a new semantic distinction to its meanings, often to match phonetic differences. For example, in regions in the United States in which the South Midlands dialect is in contact with northern speech varieties, although the word *greasy* may have two originally synonymous pronunciations, one with /s/ [grísi] and one with /z/ [grízi] many speakers came to assign distinct meanings to these variants. The one with /s/, for them, refers to a situation in which something has grease on it – as automotive grease in a garage or on a mechanic; the one with /z/ has a more negative connotation, referring to something unpleasantly slick or oily, such as in the expression *greasy spoon* [grízi spún]. See **lexical change**.

semanticization   Incorporation of inferred meanings into the conventional meaning of words, for example, *supposed to* 'presumed to' > 'probably is' > 'should'. See also **lexicalization**.

Semitic   A **language family** of the Near East and North Africa, commonly held to be a member of the larger **Afroasiatic** phylum. Semitic languages include the following: Arabic, Hebrew, Akkadian, Phoenician and Aramaic with those of the Ethiopian branch of Semitic including Amharic, Ge'ez, Tigrinya, Tigre, and many others.

shared aberrancy   A morphological or grammatical irregularity or abnormality shared by related or potentially related **languages**. **Historical linguists** place a high value on shared irregularities – shared aberrant structures in languages being assessed as potentially related genetically. It was a criterion of **genetic relationship** much prized by Antoine Meillet. Thus, in **Indo-European**, the irregularities in the paradigm of the verb *to be* shared across many Indo-European languages are diagnostic evidence that they are genetically linked to one another. An example that is frequently cited is that of the peculiar suppletive pattern shared in the comparatives and superlatives in English *good, better, best* and German *gut, besser, best,* said to be so unusual as to defy chance and borrowing as possible explanations. See also **submerged feature**.

shared innovation   A change that shows a departure from some trait or traits of the **proto-language** and is shared exclusively by a set of related languages. Shared innovation is the only generally accepted criterion for **subgrouping**. It is assumed that a shared innovation is the result of a change that took place in a single **daughter language** that subsequently diversified into daughters of its own, each of which inherited the results of the change. The innovation is thus shared by the descendants of this intermediate parent but is not shared by related languages in other subgroups of the family since they do not descend from the intermediate parent that underwent the change that the more closely related languages share through inheritance from their more immediate parent. For example, Proto-Yuman *č is retained as such in northern Yuman languages; however, the southern Yuman languages share the innovatation *č > t, for example in Mohave, Quechan, Havasupai ʔič- 'unspecified object prefix', Cocopa t-, Diegueño t-, Kiliwa t- 'unspecified object prefix; plural object prefix'. See also **shared retention, subgrouping.**

shared retention   A trait of a **proto-language** that is inherited by different **daughter languages**, shared from the proto-language regardless of whether the daughter languages that have it belong to the same **subgroup** or not. Shared retentions indicates nothing about the internal **subgrouping** among related languages within a **language family**. For example, Proto-Yuman *č is retained as such in 'northern' Yuman languages but not in the southern Yuman languages that regularly share the innovated rule *č > t. Unlike the term 'Southern' Yuman, defined by the shared innovation seen here, the designation 'northern' is merely geographic; notably, while Mohave, Maricopa and Quechan belong to the *Colorado River* sub-group, Havasupai belongs to the *Pai* or *Arizona* sub-group along with Walapai, Yavapai and Pa'ipai (actually spoken in Baja California, Mexico). The Colorado and the Pai sub-groups are no closer to one another than they are to the Southern group. See also **shared innovation.**

shift   see **semantic displacement, sound change, mechanisms of semantic change**

shortening   see clipping

simplicity   see simplification

simplification   A historical change that results in a perceived reduction of complexity in a language form or a linguistic system. For example, the Proto-Romance stressed vowel system included /i, e, ɛ, u, o, ɔ, a/; in Ibero-Romance, Portuguese preserves this system, but Spanish, on the other hand, has simplified the system by removing the contrast between the open or lax and the close or tense mid vowels, namely, /ɛ, ɔ/ and their closed analogs /e, o/, respectively. However, the removal of the open vowels introduced the complexity of a new set of diphthongs: ɛ > yé (as in *pie* 'foot') and ɔ > wé (as in *pueblo*).

Sino-Caucasian   see Dené-Caucasian, Dené-Sino-Caucasian

Sino-Tibetan   A very large **language family** of central and southeast Asia. It has two large branches, the Tibeto-Burman languages (some of which are Bodo, Garo, Burmese, Tibetan, Kachin and Karen) and Chinese languages (including Cantonese, Mandrin, Yue, Wu, Hakka and Fukien(ese). Sometimes earlier called **Indo-Chinese**.

Siouan (also often called **Siouan-Catawban, Catawba-Siouan**)   A relatively large **language family**, primarily across the Great Plains, spread from Canada to Mississipi and South Carolina. Some Siouan languages are Crow, Hidatsa, Mandan, Lakota, Osage, Quapaw, Chiwere, Biloxi, Ofo, Tutelo and Catawba. The proposed, though mostly unaccepted, **Macro-Siouan distant**

genetic relationship would link Siouan with **Caddoan** or **Iroquoian,** or both.

sister language   A **language** that is related to another language by virtue of having descended from the same common ancestor (**proto-language**); language that belongs to the same **language family** as another language. See also **daughter language.**

Slavic (sometimes called **Slavonic** languages)   A subfamily of **Indo-European.** Some Slavic languages are Russian, Ukranian, Czech, Slovak, Sorbian, Polish, Kashubian, Slovenian, Serbo-Croatian, Bulgarian, Macedonian and Old Church Slavonic (whose role is important to the history of the family, though agreement on its interpretation has not yet been reached).

socio-historical linguistics   The application of the findings and methods of sociolinguistics to **historical linguistic** questions; sociolinguistic investigation in historical (non-contemporary) contexts, such as the application of sociolinguistics to variation and change in Old English. The concept of socio-historical linguistics was made known by Romaine (1982).

sociolinguistics (and language change)   see **apparent time study, change in progress, real-time study, socio-historical linguistics, variable, variation, Weinreich–Labov–Herzog model**

softening   Another term for **lenition** or **weakening.** In another sense, a **sound change** that results in **palatalization,** particularly palatalization as a secondary manner of articulation. See also **velar softening.**

sound change (also called **phonological change**)   A change in pronunciation; the process by which sounds change their phonetic nature and phonological systems change.

sound correspondence (also called **correspondence set**)   In effect, a set of 'cognate' sounds; the sounds found in the related words in cognate sets that correspond regularly among related language because they descend from a common ancestral sound. In the **comparative method** one seeks **regular sound correspondences** across sets of **cognates** in the **daughter languages** as a necessary step prior to the **reconstruction** of the proto-sounds from which each sound correspondence derives.

sound law   see **sound change**

sound symbolism   A direct association in a **language** between sounds and meaning, where the meaning typically involves the semantic traits of 'size' or 'shape'. Size–shape sound symbolism is related to **expressive** (or iconic) **symbolism** in general, though sound symbolism can become part of a language's structural resources. The relationship between sound and meaning, assumed to be arbitrary in ordinary words, is not arbitrary in instances of sound symbolism. For example, in English, lengthened vowels can be used to indicate an emotive/expressive sense of intensity or size, as in instances in which attempts to write them are given as, for example, 'it was soooo ugly', 'it was reeeaaally wonderful', 'it was biiig and looong'.   Nevertheless, a vowel length opposition is not a formal grammatical marker of bigger versus smaller things in English grammar, though it is in some languages.

Productive sound symbolism is attested in numerous languages; for example, in Kiliwa, as in other Yuman languages (Arizona, California, Baja California, Mexico), there is a three-member, symbolic consonantal alternation series: *n, l and r*, for a semantic continuum of intensity or size, from the smallest and least intense to a neutral size and intensity, and beyond, to the largest and most intense, as in *tyin* 'tiny circular/round', *tyil* 'normal size circular/round', *tyir* 'large, spherical'; *pan* 'luke-warm', *pal* 'hot', *par* 'extremely hot' (Mixco 2000a, 2000b). Similarly, in Lakota (Siouan) there are series of alternating sibilants and fricatives, *z, ž, s, š* and *x*, seen in *waza* 'temporarily disturbed surface', *waža* 'per-manently disturbed surface', *baxa* 'twisted, crumpled'; *mnuza* 'crunching (walking on snow)', *mnuža* 'crunch-ing (walking on gravel)', *mnuxa* 'crunching (walking on a particulate, brittle mass, e.g. shells or bones)' (Boas and Deloria (1941: 16).

Regular **sound correspondences** can have exceptions in cases in which sound symbolism is involved, and this can complicate **historical linguistic** investigations, including **reconstructions** by the **comparative method** and proposals of **distant genetic relationship**. See also **onomatopoeia**.

South Asian linguistic area (also sometimes called **Indian linguistics area** or the **Indian subcontinent linguistics area**) A **linguistic area** that consists of **languages** belonging to several **language families** of the Indian subcontinent, among which are Indo-Aryan, Dravidian, Munda and Tibeto-Burman. Traits shared among them are as follows: (1) retroflex consonants, particularly retroflex stops; (2) absence of prefixes (accept in Munda); (3) presence of a dative–subject construction (that is, dative–experiencer, as in Hindi *mujhe maaluum thaa* 'I knew it' [*mujhe* 'to me' + know + Past]); (4) Subject–Object–Verb (SOV) basic word order, including postpositions; (5) absence of a verb 'to have'; (6) 'conjunctive or absolutive participles' (tendency for subordinate clauses to have non-finite verbs (that is, participles) and to be preposed; for example, relative clauses precede the nouns they modify; (7) morphological causatives; (8) so-called 'explicator compound verbs (a special auxiliary from a limited set is said to complete the sense of the immediately preceding main verb, and the two verbs together refer to a single event, as, for example, Hindi *le jaanaa* 'to take [away]' ['take' + 'go']); and (9) sound symbolic forms based on reduplication, often with *k* suffixed (for example in Kota, a Dravidian language: *kad-kadk* '[heart] beats fast with guilt or worry'; *a:nk-a:nk* 'to be very strong [of man, bullock], very beautiful [of woman]'). Some of these proposed areal features are not limited to the Indian sub-continent, but can be found also in neighboring languages (for example, SOV basic word order is found throughout much of Eurasia and northern Africa) and in languages in many other parts of the world. Some of the traits are not necessarily independent of one another (for example, languages with SOV basic word order tend also to have non-finite (participial) subordinate clauses, especially relative clauses, and not to have prefixes). (Emeneau 1956, 1980, Masica 1976.)

South Caucasian   see **Kartvelian**

speaker-innovation James Milroy (1992: 200) distinguishes between speaker-innovation and linguistic change. He distinguishes **innovators** ('marginal' persons with weak ties to more than one group who form a bridge between groups) from *early adopters* ('relatively central to the group') (p. 184); the former are associated with 'innovations' that become 'change' only when

taken up by early adopters, from whom the inno-
vation/change 'diffuses to the group as a whole' (p. 184).

specialization   see **narrowing, grammaticalization**

spelling pronunciation   Pronunciation based on the spelling
of a word rather than on its historically inherited form,
also linguistic change based on such pronunciations.
For example, many pronounce *often* with /t/, influenced
by the spelling with 't', though historically the word had
no /t/.

spirantization   see **fricativization**

split (opposite of a **merger**)   A kind of **sound change** in
which a phoneme splits into two or more phonemes in a
language. An axiom of historical phonology is that *splits
follow mergers* – the sounds in question do not themselves change physically; phonetically they stay the same,
the merger of other sounds in their environment causes
the phonemic status of the sounds involved to change
from being predictable, conditioned, variants of sounds
(allophonic) to unpredictable, contrastive, distinctive
sounds (phonemic) that contrast to produce meaning
differences in words. A case in point is the rise of **umlaut**,
the fronting of back vowels when followed by a front
vowel or glide (*i, e* or *j*) (usually in the next syllable).
Initially, proto-Germanic singular and plural nouns
showed the same root vowels: **mu:s-* 'mouse' and
*mu:s-i 'mice', **fo:t* 'foot' and **fo:t-i* 'feet'. Subsequently, these root vowels were umlauted under the
influence of the front vowel in the plural suffix: **mu:s-*
'mouse' but **mü:s-i* 'mice', **fo:t* 'foot' but **fö:t-i* 'feet'.
Finally, with the loss of final-*i*, the conditioning environment for *ü* as an allophone of *u* and of *ö* as an allophone

of *u* was no longer present; the front vowels were no longer predictable variants of the back vowels in the umlaut context; consequently, these vowels split distinct phonemes, yielding in this example four contrasting phonemes, as in: **mu:s-* 'mouse' and **mü:s* 'mice', **fo:t* 'foot' and **fö:t* 'feet'. See also **primary split, secondary split**.

splitter (opposite of **lumper**)   A linguist thought to be reluctant to accept proposals of **distant genetic relationship**, particularly without compelling evidence to support the proposal. The opposite of **splitter** is **lumper**.

sporadic change   Any irregular change, particularly a **sound change**. Typically, only one or a few forms are affected by a sporadic change. An example is the loss of /r/ in Old English *spræc* 'speech, language', giving modern *speech*, which happened only in this word, not in others, such as *spring*, *spry*, *spree* (and is preserved in the German cognate *Sprache* 'speech, language'). Changes of *metathesis*, *haplology* and *dissimilation* are sometimes sporadic.

Sprachbund   see **areal linguistics**

spread zone   Johanna Nichols' term for an area of low density where a single language or family occupies a large range, and where diversity does not build up with immigration but is reduced by language shift and language spreading. Conspicuous spread zones include the grasslands of central Eurasia, central and southern Australia, northern Africa, and the Great Basin of the western United States. (Nichols [1992], 1997: 369.)

Stammbaum   see **family tree**

standard language   A codified **variety** generally accepted as the correct or most appropriate form of the language, typically used in formal settings, writing and for education. The standard language in many cases is superimposed over regional **dialects**, with the standard having official functions and prestige and the local varieties serving as the **vernacular**. The routes to **standardization** have been different for various languages. Standardization for some languages arose from the dominant variety in politically important centers, London for English, Paris for French and Toledo and Madrid for Spanish. Standardization involved significant deliberate language planning on the part of governments, educational bodies and language academies for other languages, for example, Finnish (based on deliberate combinations of both the Eastern and Western dialects), Norwegian (with two standard varieties) and Turkish. In other cases, the standard language reflects the writings of important intellectuals, as in the case of Estonian, German and Italian. In still others, the standard is based on a body of sacred texts, as in the case of Standard Arabic, based on the Arabic of the Qur'an.

standardization   Development of a **standard language**.

stigma, stigmatization   see **covert prestige, overt prestige, prestige**

stock   Sometimes, particularly in older writing, used as equivalent to **family tree**, a translation equivalent of German **Stammbaum**. More frequently, 'stock' is used in the sense of a **genetic unit** (**clade, descent group**) with great **time depth** or of one larger than a typical **language family**, for example a language family that includes several other (sub)families as its daughters; however, 'stock' frequently implies not just large-scale family groupings but also proposed **distant linguistic relationships** that are not (yet) demonstrated, that is, hypotheses of remotely related languages in larger-scale proposed families. Johanna Nichols (1992) uses the term to mean 'a maximal reconstructable clade [genetic unit], e.g. the oldest families displaying regular sound correspondences and amenable to Neogrammarian comparative method ... The oldest known stocks are about 6000 years old: e.g. Indo-European, Uralic, Austronesian' (Nichols 1997: 362–3). See also **macro-family**.

strengthening (also called **fortition**, sometimes more rarely **hardening**)   Any of various kinds of **sound changes** that, loosely defined, share the notion that after the change the resulting sound is somehow 'stronger' in articulation than the original sound was. Some strengthening changes are **affrication, gemination, spirantization** of glides, change of fricatives or glides to stops or affricates, and consonant insertions of various sorts.

Sturtevant's paradox   The observation attributed to Edgar Sturtevant (1917) that **sound change** is regular but produces irregularity; *analogical change* is irregular but produces *regularity*. For example, when, in earlier English, *brother* pluralized to *brethren*, a regular sound change (**umlaut**) in vowels produced a paradigmatic alternation, or 'irregularity': *brother/brethren*. Subsequently, an analogical change irregularly targeting this particular *brother/brethren* 'irregularity' (and not others such as *child/children* or *ox/oxen*), produced the 'regular' *brother/brothers* (with no vowel alternation in the stem) akin to *sister/sisters*. See **analogy, regularity hypothesis.**

subfamily   see **subgroup, subgrouping**

subgroup (also called **subfamily, branch**) A group of **languages** within a **language family** that are more closely related to each other than to other languages of that family. Also called **subfamily, branch.** See also **subgrouping.**

subgrouping   The internal **classification of languages** within a **language family,** typically represented in a **family tree;** the determination of which **sister languages** are more closely related to one another within a language family, that is, the working out of the **subgroups** (**branches, subfamilies**). A **subgroup** is a group of languages within a language family that are more closely related to each other than to other languages of that family. Larger-scale language families can include smaller-scale families among their branches as their subgroups. The principal criterion for subgrouping, for determining which languages of a family belong more closely together, is **shared innovation. Shared retentions** are of little value for subgrouping.

submerged feature   Edward Sapir's term for idiosyncratic shared traits of grammar among remotely related languages so unusual they deny chance and borrowing as possible explanations for why they are shared, thus constituting evidence of a **genetic relationship** among the languages that share them. The term comes from Sapir's (1925) article that attempted to show that Subtiaba is a 'Hokan' language, repeatedly cited as a model of how **distant genetic relationships** can be approached –

ironically, since Subtiaba proved to be an **Otomanguean** language, not a **Hokan** language (Campbell 1997: 157–8, 208, 211, 292, 296–8, 325). The often cited passage from this article is:

> When one passes from a language to another that is only remotely related to it, say from English to Irish or from Haida to Hupa or from Yana to Salinan, one is overwhelmed at first by the great and obvious differences of grammatical structure. As one probes more deeply, however, significant resemblances are discovered which weigh far more in a genetic sense than the discrepancies that lie on the surface and that so often prove to be merely secondary dialectic developments which yield no very remote historical perspective. In the upshot it may appear, and frequently does appear, that the most important grammatical features of a given language and perhaps the bulk of what is conventionally called its grammar are of little value for the remoter comparison, which may rest largely on **submerged features** that are of only minor interest to a descriptive analysis. (Sapir 1925: 491–2, emphasis added.)

What Sapir intended by 'submerged features' is illustrated in his example: 'Thus, Choctaw la^nsa 'scar'/mi^nsa "scarred" is curiously reminiscent of such alternations as Subtiaba *daša* "grass"/*maša* "to be green" and suggests an old nominal prefix *l*' (Sapir 1925: 526).

Interpretations of precisely what Sapir meant by 'submerged features' have varied, though most understand his usage to mean idiosyncratic, irregular facts emphasized in language comparisons, essentially equivalent to Meillet's **shared aberrancy**. See **shared aberrancy**.

subphonemic change   see **sound change**

substratum (< Latin *substratum* 'underlayer') (also **substrate**)
When an earlier language influences a later language
which moves into its territory (causing its extinction or
becoming dominant), the earlier language is called a
substratum. In **language contact**, a term applied to the
effects on linguistic structures (phonological, morphological, semantic or syntactic) transferred from the
earlier language to the one that arrived later in the same
territory. In some cases substatum influence can be
outright lexical or structural loans from the earlier
language to the later arriving language. The propensity
of the Tuscan dialect of Italian to fricativize syllable-
initial /k/ > [x] is often said to be a lingering effect of the
phonology of the Etruscan language that preceded Latin
in that region. Similarly, the vigesimal numerals of
modern French of France (in which 'forty' is structurally
two twenties and 'eighty' four twenties, and so on) are
seen as a substrate effect of Gaulish (Celtic). The
tendency of some Andean dialects of American Spanish
to preserve the palatal lateral /lʸ/ in contrast to the
majority of Latin American Spanish dialects that
prefer the glide /y/ is seen as propitiated by heavy
Quechua–Spanish bilingualism in that region. Quechua
has an /l/-/lʸ/ phonemic contrast. See also **adstratum**,
superstratum.

Sumerian An important language **isolate** of the ancient
Near East, the language of ancient Sumer, spoken in
Southern Mesopotamia from about 3100 BC. Sumerian
was replaced by Akkadian as a spoken language around
2000 BC, but continued to be used as a sacred, cere-
monial and scientific language until about 100 BC.

superstratum (also **superstrate**) In **language contact**, a
superstratum language (or **superstrate** language) is the

language of an invading people that is imposed on an indigenous population and contributes features to the indigenous people's language. This takes place in the situation in which a more powerful or less prestigious language comes to influence a more local, less powerful or prestigious language, as in cases of conquest or political domination. Often the superstrate language does not survive indefinitely in the area, as for example in the case of the invading Visigoths who ruled in Spain from 412 until 711, whose Germanic language left many loanwords and some other linguistic influences on Spanish, but did not itself survive there.

suppletion   The use of two or more originally unconnected forms (roots, stems) in the inflection of a single lexical item, for example, *go / went*, where originally *went* was not part of the tenses of 'to go' but rather was the past tense of *wend*, which was taken over as the past of 'to go' and incorporated into its inflectional paradigm. Exceptions to linguistic patterns are often seen as suppletive.

svarabhakti   see **anaptyxis**

swamping   Situation in which traits from the **dialect** of the majority in the population are accepted and, consequently, features from minority dialects that are not shared with the majority dialect are suppressed. This can also hold where a majority **language** pushes out a minority language. Swamping takes place when the cumulative weight of the speech of subsequent immigrants is so great that it takes over or pushes out traits from earlier **varieties** that are not found in the dialect of the new incoming majority. Again, whole languages can be pushed out, swamped, when the language of subsequent immigrants who come in great numbers is taken over. Swamping is, in a sense, the opposite of the **founder effect**. (Lass 1990.)

synchronic linguistics   see **synchrony, diachronic linguistics**

synchrony (the opposite of **diachrony**)   Occurrence at the same time; when applied to language, synchrony means looking at a language at a single point in time, often the present, but not necessarily so. For example, a grammatical description of present-day French would be a synchronic grammar, as would a grammar written of Old French if it represented a single point in time.

syncope (< Greek *sunkopé* 'a cutting away', from *sun* 'with' + *kopé* 'cut, beat')   **Sound change** in which a vowel is lost (deleted) from the interior of a word (not initially or finally), as, for example, in English *family* > *fam'ly*; *memory* > *mem'ry*; Latin *pópulu* > Proto-Romance *pɔp'lu* > Spanish *pueblo*, French *peuple*; Latin *fãbulare* > proto-Romance *fab'lare* 'confabulate, to tells tall tales, fables' > Spanish *(h)ablar* 'to speak', Portuguese *falar* 'to speak'. The **loss** (deletion) of internal consonants is not usually called syncope, though sometimes it is, as in the following Swedish examples: *norðman* > *norman*, *norðr-vegi > *norwegi 'Norway, *Västby* 'west village' > *Väsby* (Wessén 1969: 68).

syncretism   Change in which a single linguistic form comes to cover different functions previously covered by two or more separate forms; for example, in former times the English word *span* was the past tense form of *spin* while *spun* was the past participle but now the two have syncretized to *spun* 'past' and 'past participle'. Examples of case syncretism are well known in some **Indo-**

European languages. For example, in **languages** of the Balkans the formerly distinct dative and genitive cases have merged to one in form and function, as in Romanian *fetei* 'to the girl' or 'the girl's'.

synecdoche (< Greek *sunekdokhé* 'inclusion')   A kind of **semantic change**, often considered a kind **metonymy**, that involves a part-to-whole relationship in which a term with more comprehensive meaning is used for a less comprehensive meaning or vice versa. In synecdoche a part (or quality) is used to refer to the whole, or the whole is used to refer to part, for example *hand* was extended to include also 'hired hand, employed worker'. The term originates in the conceptual imagery of classical rhetoric, as in *a good soul* for *a person*, *the radio said* for a *person broadcast on the radio*, *the press arrived* for *journalists arrived* (individually or collectively). Further examples include Spanish *boda* 'marriage vows' > 'a wedding' and German *Bein* 'bone' > 'leg' (compare the English cognate *bone*).

A special kind of synecdoche is **displacement** (or **ellipsis**) in which a word absorbs part or all of the meaning of a word with which it occurs in linear order, as in *capital city* > *capital*, *private soldier* > *private*. Historical examples of displacement are: French *succès favorable* 'favorable result, outcome' > *succès* 'a success' (compare English *success*, borrowed from French, contrasted with Spanish *suceso* 'an occurrence, incident, outcome').

synonymy (< Greek *sun-* 'with', *onoma* 'name') The identity or near identity of semantic reference or meaning for two or more morphemes, words or sentences that are otherwise phonologically distinct; one type is lexical synonymy, for example, *animals/fauna*, *plants/vegetation/flora*, *pair/couple/two*, *leaves/foliage*, *forest/woods*.

An example of (near) synonymy in syntax is that holding between active and passive sentences, for example, *the cat ate the mouse/the mouse was eaten by the cat*. The choice of synonyms can be constrained by stylistic concerns or may respond to a variety of other contextual factors.

syntactic blend   see **blending**

syntactic borrowing   Process by which a **language** acquires a syntactic structure through contact with another language. Thus, many American Indian languages, such as Nahuatl and Yaqui (both Uto-Aztecan languages), that once lacked conjunctions have borrowed them from Spanish, creating new subordinate and conjoined constructions. Others, like Kiliwa (Yuman family, Baja California, Mexico), may have innovated them out of native materials under the pressure of **language contact** with Spanish (Mixco 1985). Syntactic borrowing is considered one of only three **mechanisms of syntactic change**. See also **areal linguistics, borrowing**.

syntactic change (also sometimes called **grammatical change**) Change in the syntax of a language, that is, in the order or relationship among words and structural elements in phrases and sentences; change in 'grammar' or in the morphosyntax of a language. It is argued that there are only three **mechanisms of syntactic change: reanalysis, extension,** and **borrowing** (Harris and Campbell 1995).

syntactic reconstruction   Reconstruction of syntax by the **comparative method** or **internal reconstruction**. Opinions vary over whether or to what extent syntactic reconstruction may be possible, though significant aspects of the syntax of various **proto-languages** have been reconstructed successfully in several cases, in Finno-Ugric, **Indo-European,** Kartvelian, Mayan etc. (Campbell 1990, Harris and Campbell 1995).

synthesis   see **synthetic languages**

synthetic languages   In language **typology,** one of four morphological types proposed in 1818 by A. W. Schlegel, characterized by a high morpheme-to-word ratio, a tendency involving a variety of *portmanteau* inflectional morphemes (that is, one single unit with multiple components of meaning). The subject–tense/mood/ aspect agreement suffixes in Spanish, for example, *habl-o* 'I speak', carry multiple meanings: /-o/ '*first person, singular, indicative mood, present tense*'. See **fusional language, inflectional language.**

systematic correspondence, systematic sound correspon-dence   see **sound correspondence**

☐ T ☐

taboo avoidance (also called **euphemism**)   Process that can be a factor in **lexical change,** in that a term becomes unacceptable in certain social settings. Thus, in many traditional societies of the Americas and Australia, use of any word that evokes the name or memory of the deceased is avoided and usually replaced. In the Hua language of Papua-New Guinea, men avoid the word for 'axe' totally in the presence of certain female relatives due to its perceived sexual imagery (Haiman 1979). In Victorian England, many terms referring to or evoking body parts were avoided because of their potential for an improper sexual connotation. Thus, the euphemism *limb* replaced *leg.* Words considered blasphemous in various religions are euphemized, as in English *heck*, *golly*, *gosh*, *geez*, *dickens*, *darn*, or they are simply avoided altogether. In many hunting societies the name of feared predators receive similar treatment, for example *bear* > *honey* or *auntie* as in Kiliwa (Yuman), Proto-Yuman **mx^waa tay* 'bear' (literally 'badger large') > *k^wmaqn* 'sweet one' (Mixco 1983, 1985, 2000b). In modern Western societies, in attempts towards *political correctness* (abbreviated to PC) various formerly common terms are avoided to prevent injury or insult in the domains of gender, religion, race, ethnicity and so on.

Tai   A family of languages from Southeast Asia and southern China, spoken by more than 80 million people. Some Tai languages are: Thai, Lao, Shan and Ahom, and there are numerous others. All Tai languages are tonal. Tai is usually held to be a subgroup of the larger **Tai-Kadai** genetic grouping.

Tai-Kadai   A large **language family**, generally but not universally accepted, of languages located in Southeast Asia and southern China. The family includes **Tai**, Kam-Sui, Kadai and various other languages. The genetic relatedness of several proposed Tai-Kadai languages is not yet settled.

tapping   see **flapping**

taxonomy, linguistic taxonomy   Term used by some to refer to **genetic classification** of languages. See also **classification, subgrouping**.

teleology of language change   Goal-oriented change in language, any change thought to achieve a purpose or goal, such as, for example, changes thought to facilitate ease of comprehension or of production of the language.

In philosophy a distinction is sometimes made between 'teleology of purpose' – the intentionality, purposiveness or goal-directedness exhibited in the behavior or actions of people, other organisms or machines – and 'teleology of function', the contribution that the presence or absence of some object makes to some state of affairs being attained or maintained. In spite of opposition to teleological explanations of linguistic change, many traditional forms of **explanation of linguistic change** are markedly teleological in character; for example **avoidance of homophony**, treatments of **push chains**, changes to attain greater prestige or signal group membership and so forth, along with appeals to **morphological conditioning** of **sound change**, various proposed therapeutic changes and so on. Also, though numerous scholars may object to teleological explanations, some changes explained by 'teleology of purpose' are not controversial. Language is, after all, used by humans, who, through intention and intervention, bring about some purposive changes in language; there are, for instance, abundant examples of attempts to attain prestige, show local identity, identify with a particular group and so on that have lead to purposeful selection of certain variants over others that condition change in language – for example, the centralization of diphthongs on Martha's Vineyard, the Northern Cities Vowel Shift, presence or absence of non-prevocalic 'r' in New York City etc.

One objection to teleological explanations involves the claim that teleology reverses the normal order of cause before effect (that it is *post hoc*); however, an appeal to goals, functions, motives, purposes, aims, drives, needs or intentions does not require inversion of the normal cause-before-effect order. The problem is not the reversal of cause and effect; it is, rather, about the proper identification of the cause. In many changes it is clear enough that the intentions, desires, beliefs (to affiliate with some group, to attain higher social status etc.) precede the linguistic behavior, and the selection of linguistic traits (variables and variants of variables) is indeed human choice in order to attain these ends (see **invisible hand theory**).

Chain shifts, for example, can be seen as instances in which the teleology of *function* is involved, where the presence or absence of some object contributes to some state of affairs being attained or maintained. To say that the chain shift takes place in order to preserve phonemic contrasts or to maintain lexical distinctions by avoiding the many homonyms that would result from merger is not the same as saying that the preservation of these distinctions causes chain shifting. Preservation is not the cause, but the goal. The cause is the state of affairs in which such changes are required or helpful in maintaining the word distinctions, and this state of affairs existed prior to the chain shifting changes (the effect).

Another objection to teleological explanations is the claim that they inappropriately attribute human characteristics to other things. But language is used by humans and some linguistic changes are clearly due to human intentions (teleology of purpose), as mentioned above. In these sorts of changes, the objection of inappropriate attribution of human characteristics does not hold. In the examples involving teleology of function, also, no misguided attribution of human characteristics need be involved. These examples do not refer to any intentions, beliefs or desires of the language in question, but rather refer only to some state of affairs in which certain events or entities would in fact contribute to the goal of keeping distinctions. So long as the states of affairs can be identified reliably, the usual objections to teleological explanation do not hold (Campbell and Ringen 1981: 63–4).

tensing   Sound change in which a vowel becomes tensed. The opposite of tensing is **laxing**. (In comparison to lax sounds, tense sounds involve greater effort of the muscles in the vocal tract and more movement of the vocal tract.)

therapeutic change   Change that is assumed to help alleviate (or even also perhaps to prevent in some views) the negative consequences of other changes on the structure or lexicon of the language undergoing the deleterious changes. For example, Standard Spanish freely allows independent pronouns optionally to be absent, since the bound pronominal suffixes on verbs can indicate the subject (for example, *ando* 'I walk', *andas* 'you walk', *andamos* 'we walk'), and in connected discourse the independent pronouns are usually absent. However, in varieties of Caribbean Spanish, the independent pronouns *tú* 'you (familiar)', *usted* 'you (formal)', *él* 'he', and *ella* 'she' occur much more frequently than in other varieties of Spanish. Setting aside the possibility of influence from contact with English, therapeutic compensation is a proposed explanation (though not one accepted by all scholars of the topic) for this change to fix things up in the wake of disruptive sound changes. In these varieties of Spanish, final *s* changes very frequently to *h* and goes further to Ø, leaving verb forms that are quite distinct in Standard Spanish, such as *andas* 'you walk' versus *anda* 'he/she walks', no longer distinct if the final *s* is not realized. The **loss** of this morphological distinction through the **sound change** deleting the final *s* is compensated for by the use of the independent pronouns, especially *tú* 'you (familiar)', where they are needed to help maintain the formal difference in verbs (now *tú anda* 'you walk' versus *él anda* 'he walks' in the colloquial language). This greater use of *tú* to compensate for the lost *-s* pronominal suffix parallels the change in French; French was once like modern Standard Spanish, with *vas* 'you go' versus *va* 'he/she goes', but as a result of sound changes that affected final consonants in French, the *-s* of the 'you' forms was completely lost and in French today the independent pronouns are obligatory, /tu va/ 'you go' (spelled *tu vas*) versus /il va/ 'he goes'. The claim is, then, that the use of independent pronouns was made obligatory to compensate for the meaning contrast that would otherwise be lost with the loss of the final *-s* of second person. See also **teleology of language change**.

Thracian   An extinct and poorly attested **Indo-European** language once spoken in the Balkans.

time depth   The length of time since some linguistic event took place, typically used in connection with the time since a **proto-language** split up (or is hypothesized to have split up) into **daughter languages**, for example, Proto-Mayan is said to have been unified until 2200 BC, thus having a time depth of 4,200 years; the time depth of **Proto-Indo-European** is generally held to be around 6,000 years (4000 BC), though opinions vary on this.

time-depth ceiling (on the **comparative method**)   The assumption that the comparative method can only reach back in time a certain distance and becomes ineffective after some 6,000 or 8,000 or 10,000 years, depending on the opinions of different scholars. This is based on the observation that the most successful and least contentious **proto-language** reconstructions have not succeeded in extending beyond a **time-depth** of between six and eight millennia before the present. Evidence for and conclusions about **reconstructions** beyond these dates tend to be tenuous and controversial due to the scarcity and lower reliability of the supporting data. As more time goes by, more changes in the sounds and grammar of related languages accumulate and more lexical loss and replacement takes place so that, logically, a point is reached at which insufficient material inherited from the original ancestor language remains intact or remains sufficiently unchanged for it to be recognizable any longer as cognate, thus rendering the comparative method inapplicable. What the date at which this happens may be, and whether it is similar across languages, is unknown, though, as mentioned, attempted reconstructions beyond around 6,000 to 8,000 years ago have not proven successful so far.

Tocharian A and B (also sometimes **Tokharian**) Extinct **Indo-European** languages of the Tocharian branch that were preserved in ancient Buddhist manuscripts uncovered by twentieth-century archeologists in the deserts of Chinese Turkestan, in Xinjiang Province and the Uighur Autonomous Region. There are two **languages**: an eastern one and a western one; the former is also known as *Agnean* and the latter as *Kuchean*. Tocharian reduced the three Proto-Indo-European stop series (voiceless, voiced and voiced aspirates) to one; it is also known for its conservative verb system.

Tonkawa An **extinct language isolate** of Texas. Proposals to link Tonkawa with the languages of the **Coahuiltecan** or **Hokan-Coahuiltecan** hypotheses have not generally been accepted.

tonogenesis   The development of tone; typically the process that produces tonal contrasts in a language that formerly had no phonemic tone, though the term can also be applied to the development of a new tone in a tonal language.

total assimilation   see **assimilation**

trade language, trade jargon   A simplified language used for trade and other limited contact among groups who otherwise have no common language, usually based largely on one language but often also with lexical items from other languages involved in the intergroup communication via the trade language. Examples of trade languages or trade jargons include Chinook Jargon, Mobilian Jargon and Chinese Pidgin English. See also **lingua franca, pidgin.**

transfer   In **language contact,** the acquisition of a linguistic feature not formerly part of the language from a neighboring language. See also **interference, phonetic interference.**

transition area   see **dialect geography, focal area, relic area**

transition problem   Concerned with the question, how (or by what route or routes) does language change? What intermediate stages or processes does a language go through to move from a state before the change began to the state after the change has taken place? For example, a much debated question is whether certain kinds of changes must be seen as gradual or abrupt.

transparency   The property of clarity of linguistic structures and analyses; linguistic units and constructions that are transparent are straightforward for the linguist to analyze and for children to attain in language acquisition. The opposite of transparency is *opacity*; transparent aspects of language are assumed to be easier for children to learn; opaque aspects are harder and more subject to change. A good number of scholars believe that the outcome of linguistic change tends to be in the direction of greater transparency (less opacity), all else being equal.

trisyllabic laxing   A sound change in English in which long (or tense) vowels were shortened (became lax) in polysyllabic words in which the vowel was followed by at least two more syllables, as seen in the second form in the alternations: *holy/holiday, sane/sanity, nation/ national, profound/profundity, divine/divinity*. The forms outside the environment for trisyllabic laxing (the first of the forms in these examples), because they remained long, underwent the **Great Vowel Shift**, changing the quality of the vowel.

Tsimshian   A small family of languages spoken on the coast of British Columbia and Alaska, including Nass-Gitksan and Coast Tsimshian.

truncation   **Sound change** in which one or more sounds, particularly of a vowel, is lost, especially at the end of words. See also **apocope**.

Tungusic   A **language family** of eastern Siberia and Manchuria to which Manchu, Even, Evenki (Tungus) and others belong. Tungusic is often linked with the **Altaic hypothesis**, but most specialists do not accept Altaic as a valid genetic grouping.

Tupian (Tupían)   A large **language family** with member **languages** spoken in Brazil, Paraguay, Bolivia, Argentina, Colombia and Venezuela. One of its members is the very large **Tupí-Guaraní** subfamily, with several languages in its own right. Paraguayan Guaraní is best known, one of the official languages of Paraguay, with some 3 million speakers. Some other branches of Tupian are Mundurukú, Juruna, Arikem and Tuparí, Mondé, as well as the widespread trade language Lingua Geral Amazônica or Nheengatu (simplified version of Tupinambá).

Turanian   A term no longer used for a now abandoned language classification that, in various versions, is thought to have embraced the **Uralic** and so-called **Altaic** languages, but in fact essentially included all the non-**Sino-Tibetan** languages of Asia. This name is based on Turan, part of Inner Asia that was the hypothetical homeland of the Turks. This was not a classification based on comparative linguistics, but rather represented the non-**Indo-European** and non-**Semitic** languages that shared agglutinative structure, which Müller held to be associated with a particular stage in the assumed uni-linear social evolution of society, also called 'nomadic languages' (Müller 1855).

Turkic   A family of about thirty languages, spoken across central Asia from China to Lithuania. The family has two branches: Chuvash (of the Volga region) and the non-Chuvash Turkic branch of relatively closely related languages. Some of the Turkic languages are Azeri, Kyrgyz, Tatar, Crimean Tatar, Uighur, Uzbek, Yakut, Tuvan and Tofa. Turkic is often assigned to the '**Altaic**' hypothesis, though specialists have largely abandoned Altaic.

typological change   see **typology**

typology, language typology   The classification of languages
in terms of their structural characteristics. The typol-
ogies that have received the most attention are those that
have attempted broad classifications based on a number
of interrelated features. There are many possible ways
of categorizing languages according to their structure.
Historically, languages were often classified according to
their morphological tendencies as **isolating, inflecting** or
agglutinating. Typology as practiced today investigates
differences, and hence also similarities, across languages,
and is thus closely linked with the study of linguistic
universals. A joint concern of typology and universals is
with determining what are the expected correlations
among parts of a language's grammar, and hence with
determining aspects of the nature of human language in
general. Typology plays an important role in historical
linguistics in that it provides checks and balances on
what might be proposed in reconstructions or for
linguistic changes. Things known from typology to be
unlikely are avoided in **reconstructions** and postulated
changes, and when not avoided, require strong supporting evidence. On the other hand, things known from
typology to be commonplace across languages provide
less compelling evidence for family relationships among
languages since they may be due to independent development. Neither do they provide strong evidence for
subgrouping, if languages in a family can easily change
independently to acquire the commonplace traits with
no historical connection.

U

umlaut (also called **metaphony**)   Sound change (**distant assimilation**) in which a vowel is fronted under the influence of a following front vowel or glide, usually in the next syllable. Umlaut has been particularly important in the history of Germanic languages. For example, Proto-Germanic **badja* 'bed' became *bedja* by umlaut and later the **-ja* was lost in a series of changes, giving English *bed*, German *Bett*. Umlaut also left morphological alternations in Germanic languages, as, for example, in German *hand* 'hand', but *hände* [hɛnde] 'hands', where the plural *-e*, a front vowel, caused the /a/ of the root to be fronted to /ɛ/.

unconditioned sound change (also called **unconditioned phonological change**)   Sound change that occurs generally wherever the sound appears in the language in question and is not dependent on the phonetic context in which it occurs, that is, not dependent on or restricted by neighboring sounds. Unconditioned sound changes modify a sound in all contexts in which it occurs. **Grimm's Law** and the English **Great Vowel Shift** are examples of unconditioned sound changes. See also **conditioned sound change**.

unidirectional intelligibility   see **non-reciprocal intelligibility, partial intelligibilty, mutual intelligibility**

unidirectionality   In **grammaticalization**, the typical direction of change is lexical item > grammatical marker; changes in the reverse order (grammatical > lexical) are rare. Unidirectionality in grammaticalization is much debated, since the directionality is built into the very definition of grammaticalization, but, nevertheless, some counterexamples (sometimes called **degrammaticalizations**) do exist (cases of grammatical > lexical). Unidirectionality should not be confused with **directionality**, though sometimes the two are used interchangeably. Unidirectionality essentially embodies a claim that changes in the opposite direction should not occur; directionality, on the other hand, refers to the typical direction of many changes, though it makes no strong claim that examples in the opposite direction cannot or should not exist, only that they should not be common.

uniformitarianism, Uniformitarian Principle   A fundamental principle of biological, geological and linguistic sciences, which holds for linguistics that things about language that are possible today were not impossible in the past and that things that are impossible today were not possible in the past. This means that whatever is known to occur in languages today would also have been possible in earlier human languages and anything not possible in contemporary languages was equally impossible in the past, in the earlier history of any language. The Uniformitarian Principle came to linguistics from Charles Lyell's formulation of it in geology. It is valuable for **reconstruction** via the **comparative method**, where, according to the principle, nothing in reconstruction can be assumed to have been a property of some **protolanguage** if it is not possible in known languages.

univerbation   Change of a group of two or more words into a single word, as in the change in which *full* became a bound suffix in words such as *handful, mouthful* and later, *hopeful*, and as seen in the changes of *going to* and *want to* to *gonna* and *wanna*. See also **blending, amalgamation**.

unproductive (also called **frozen, fossilized** and **crystalized**) Said of linguistic elements that can no longer be utilized in new circumstances – usually said of morphemes, words or constructions that cannot combine freely with others to create new occurrences in a language, though perhaps formerly they may have been **productive** and could enter in combinations to produce new forms. For example, the plural suffix *-en* is unproductive, occurring only in frozen forms, such as *oxen, brethren, children*; it cannot combine with nouns now to create new plural forms, as *-es/-s* (productive) does, as in *cats, buses* etc. See **fossilization, productive.**

unrounding   **Sound change** in which rounding (lip-rounding) is lost from a sound, usually from a vowel but also from consonants. For example, English front rounded /y:/ and /ö:/ lost their rounding, thus the history of English *mice* and *geese* illustrates unrounding: originally /mu:s-i/ and /go:s-i/ underwent **umlaut** to become /my:si/ and /gö:si/ and eventually lost the final vowel, becoming /my:s/ and /gö:s/, which then underwent unrounding to give /mi:s/ and /ge:s/, which then underwent the **Great Vowel Shift** to give modern /mais/ 'mice' and /gis/ 'geese'.

Ural-Altaic hypothesis   A macro-family proposed in the nineteenth century but rejected today, which has as members **Uralic** and the so-called **Altaic** languages. The idea of a genetic relationships between these languages was based primarily on shared typological traits such as: (1) SOV (Subject-Object-Verb) word order, (2) **agglutinating** morphology, (3) overwhelming suffixing and (4) vowel harmony. These are commonplace, easily developing independently, as seen in many other languages of the world, and it has been hypothesized that some of these traits may be shared due to areal linguistic infuences.

Uralic   A reasonably large, well-known **language family**, that takes its name from the Ural Mountains. It extends over a vast area from Siberia to the Baltic Sea and to central Europe. Its two major branches are **Finno-Ugric** (some thirty languages) and **Samoyed** (some dozen languages). Finnish, Estonian, Hungarian and numerous others belong to Finno-Ugric. The proto-Uralic **homeland** (**Urheimat**) is postulated to have centered on the Volga River and the Ural Mountains.

Uralo-Yukaghir   The hypothesized **genetic relationship** that would link **Uralic** and **Yukaghir**.

Urheimat   The German term for **linguistic homeland**, also often used in English. See **linguistic homeland**.

Uto-Aztecan   Large family of some thirty languages extending from Oregon to Nicaragua. Nahuatl was the language of the Aztecs, also of the Toltecs, and has over 1 million speakers. Some other languages of the Southern branch of the family are Cora, Huichol, Tarahumara and Yaqui. Some members of the Northern Uto-Aztecan branch are Hopi, Ute, Shoshone, Luiseño and many others. The Proto-Uto-Aztecan homeland appears to have been in Arizona and northern Mexico, possibly extending also into southern California. (See Miller 1983, Campbell 1997: 133–8.)

$\boxed{\text{V}}$

variable (also called **linguistic variable, sociolinguistic variable**) Any linguistic element that displays *variation* or *variability*, usually correlated with variation in some aspect of society. For example, in Labov's (1970) famous study of Martha's Vineyard, the diphthongs /ay, aw/ proved to be sociolinguistic variables, where a variant with a more centralized vowel [əy, əw] correlated with the social attribute of identity with the island, a mark of *solidarity* (**covert prestige**) with the core values of the island community on the part of those who permanently resided on the island. Those who felt less local identity had a variant with less centralized vowels, [ay, aw].

Language changes often begin with variation, with alternative ways of saying the same thing. **Sociolinguistics** deals with systematic co-variation of linguistic structure (linguistic variables) with social structure, especially with the variation in language that is conditioned by social differences. Linguistic variables can be conditioned by any of a number of social attributes of the sender (speaker), the receiver (hearer) and the setting (context). Variation in a language can be conditioned by such social characteristics of the speaker as age, gender, class and social status, ethnic identity, religion, occupation etc. The variable, thus, is fundamental to discussion of most changes in progress and to understanding linguistic change in general.

variant Any of the different forms that a linguistic item (sound, word, construction etc.) can have in a language at a particular time. For example, English *economics* has the two variants, /ɛkənɔmIks/, where the first vowel is pronounced as in 'bed', and /ikənɔmɪks/ with the first vowel as in 'bead'; intervocalic /t/ after a stressed vowel in English can occasionally have two variants, depending on the speaker, for example, *Latin* as [læʔn] or [læthɪn].

variation (also called **linguistic variation**)   The occurrence of alternative linguistic forms with essentially the same linguistic content and function in a single speech community or **variety** of language. Linguistic variation is the principal subject matter of sociolinguistics, which deals with the systematic co-variation of the structure of language and social structures, especially as conditioned by social differences such as age, gender, socioeconomic status, religious affiliation, ethnicity, occupation and region. See also **variable**.

variety   Any body of human speech patterns that is sufficiently homogeneous to be analyzed linguistically and that has a sufficiently large number of linguistic elements to function in all normal contexts of communication. *Variety* is sometimes used as a sort of cover term when it is not certain whether independent **languages** or divergent **dialects** of the same language are in question or when both independent languages and non-independent dialects of other languages are talked about together. See also **lect**.

Vedic (also called **Vedic Sanskrit**)   The language of the Vedas, the earliest Hindu hymns. Traditionally, Vedic was considered the oldest recorded form of Sanskrit, earlier transmitted orally and written down after 800 BC, allegedly preserving significant archaic features of Sanskrit, though it is also argued that Vedic is not Sanskrit, but a separate language of the **Indo-Aryan** branch of **Indo-European**, closely related to Sanskrit. The Rig-Veda is earliest and the most famous collection of Sanskrit hymns, composed perhaps around 1500 BC.

velar softening   Change in which velar stops are palatalized. More particularly, also the name of the phonological process in English that deals with the alternation of velar stops with affricates and fricatives when followed by front vowels (or glides), for example, of /k/ with /s/ or /š/ (as in *critic* but *criticize*), and of /g/ with /ǰ/ (as in *colleague* but *collegial*). Many of these words are not native to English, but rather come from Latin or **Romance** languages.

vernacular   The **variety** of **language** learned in the domestic setting as one is growing up; the most typical variety one speaks when not monitoring speech and not otherwise attempting to adapt to others.

Verner's Law   A famous **sound change**, named for its discoverer, Karl Verner (1877), in which Proto-Germanic non-initial voiceless fricatives became voiced when the stress followed, rather than preceded these sounds. Verner's Law explains some seeming exceptions to **Grimm's Law**. In part of Grimm's Law, **Proto-Indo-European** voiceless stop series became voiceless fricatives in Proto-Germanic (Indo-European $*p$, $*t$, $*k$, $*k^w$ > Germanic f, θ, x, x^w respectively); however, Grimm's law holds only when these sounds are found after the vowel that carries the stress or are in word-initial position. Verner's Law accounts for apparent exceptions to Grimm's Law in which the Germanic fricatives are predictably (allophonically) *voiced* (rather than *voiceless*, as predicted in Grimm's Law) depending on the placement of the unpredictable stress in the **proto-language**, best preserved in Sanskrit, Greek and Lithuanian cognates, but later not visible in Germanic when Germanic shifted to first-syllable stress. By Grimm's law, Germanic medial voiceless fricative reflexes correspond to voiceless stops in the other languages: Old English *hēafod* 'head', Latin *caput*; Gothic *brōthar* 'brother', Ṣanskrit *bhrá:tar-*; Gothic *táihun* 'ten', Greek *déka*, Old High German *swéhar* 'father-in-law', Sanskrit *çváçurah*. However, other forms, seeming exceptions to Grimm's Law, show inter-vocalic voiced fricatives *β, *ð, *γ, as in: Gothic *sibun* 'seven', Sanskrit *saptá-*; Old English *fæðer* 'father', Sanskrit *pitár-*; Gothic *tigus* 'decade', Greek *dekás;* Old High German *swígar* 'mother-in-law'; Sanskrit *çvaçrú:h* 'mother-in-law'. Verner discovered that these cases could be explained by taking into account the placement of the original Proto-Indo-European stress. When stress *preceded* the medial fricative the latter was voiceless, but, when it followed, the medial fricative was voiced. **Grammatical alternation**, the English equivalent of German ***grammatischer Wechsel***, has to do with differences in related forms in morphological paradigms produced by Verner's Law.

vocalization   Sound change the result of which is a vowel or a more vocalic sound than before the change. For example, final 'l' of a number of English varieties is vocalized to some back vowel or glide, such as *little >* *[lɪdo], milk > [mɪwk]*.

voicing   Sound change in which a sound becomes voiced. Voicing usually takes place by **assimilation** from a neigh-boring voiced sound. A frequent voicing environment is intervocalic, for example **Romance** intervocalic voiceless stops (*p, t, k > b, d, g*), as in Vulgar Latin *ispata* 'sword' > Spanish and Portuguese *espada, (res) nata* 'born (thing) (feminine)' > Spanish, Portuguese *nada* 'nothing' and Latin *amīka* 'friend (feminine)' > Spanish, Portuguese *amiga*. Likewise, in Shoshone (Numic branch, Uto-Aztecan), *papi* 'older brother' > [páβi], *ata* 'mother's brother' > [ářa], *patsi'i* 'older sister' > [pázi'i]. Some Spanish dialects voice an /s/ contiguous to a voiced consonant, for example, *desde* [dézde] 'since', *mismo* [mízmo] 'same', *rasgo* [rázgo] 'trait'.

W

Wackernagel's Law The generalization about earlier Indo-European languages that enclitics (and sometimes other unstressed grammatical material, such as auxiliary verb forms) 'occupied the second position in the sentence' (Collinge 1985: 217). The 'law' is associated with Jacob Wackernagel (1892), though it is also credited to Delbrück's (1878) earlier work. The same tendency has been observed in numerous other languages, and often Wackernagel's Law is thought to be a general or universal tendency, where sentence second position is called 'Wackernagel's position'.

Waiilatpuan see **Cayuse-Molala**

Wakashan A medium-sized family of languages spoken mostly in British Columbia and Washington state. The Northern Wakashan branch contains Kwakiutl (Kwak'wala) with Heiltsuk (Bella Bella) and Haisla (Kitamat); Southern Wakashan, also called Nootkan, contains Nootka, Nitinat and Makah.

Wanderwort (from German *Wanderwort* 'wandering word'; also sometimes called **wandering word**) A **borrowed** word diffused across numerous language, usually with a wide geographical distribution; typically it is impossible to determine the original **donor** language from which the **loanword** in other languages originated. An example is seen in words for 'pot' across several Eurasian languages: Indo-European *pod- 'vessel, pot, box', Finno-Ugric *pata 'cauldron, pot', Dravidian *patalV 'pot'. Some associate this *Wanderwort* with the inception and spread of ceramic culture across Europe beginning as early as the sixth millennium BC. Another example is seen in the forms for 'horse' in several East Asian languages: Mongolian *morin*, Korean *mar* (< *morï*), Chinese *ma*, Japanese *uma*, Nivkh *murng*, with **Indo-European** parallels (as in English *mare*).

Watkin's Law The generalization formulated by Calvert Watkins (1962) that in verb paradigms, forms for other persons tend to change to be like the 'third person singular' verb form; the 'third person singular' form serves as the model for analogical changes in verbal morphology.

wave theory (< German *Wellentheorie*; also called the **wave model**) A model of linguistic change seen by some as an alternative to the **family tree model** but thought by others to complement the family tree model; it is intended to deal with changes due to contact among **languages** and **dialects**. According to the wave model, linguistic changes spread outward concentrically as waves on a pond do when a stone is thrown into it, becoming progressively weaker with the distance from their central point. Since later changes may not cover the same area there may be no sharp boundaries between neighboring dialects or languages; rather, the greater the distance between them, the fewer linguistic traits dialects or languages may share. See also **dialect geography**.

weakening Change in which some linguistic material (usually sounds, but potentially any linguistic entity – words, morphemes, constructions, meanings etc.) is considered to be in some way diminished, reduced, deteriorated, eroded, shortened or deleted after the change. See **lenition**.

Weinreich–Labov–Herzog model of language change (sometimes also called the **WLH-model**) A model of **language change** informed by **sociolinguistic** considerations put forward by Weinreich, Labov and Herzog (1968). In this model, five problems (or questions) are addressed: constraints, **transition, embedding, evaluation** and **actuation**. See also **actuation problem, constraints problem, embedding problem, evaluation problem** and **transition problem**.

Wellentheorie German term for **wave theory** sometimes used in English.

widening (also called **broadening, generalization**) **Semantic change** in which the range of meanings of a word increases so that the word can be used in more contexts than were appropriate for it before the change. In widening, a lexical item decreases the number of its semantic features, thereby expanding the breadth of coverage of the original meaning to a larger set of referents. For example: Latin *passer* 'sparrow' > Spanish *pájaro* '(generic) bird'; Middle English *dogge* 'canine breed' > Modern English *dog* 'generic dog (any domestic canine)'. See also **narrowing**.

Wintuan A family of languages spoken in northen California that includes Wintu, Nomlaki and Patwin. Wintuan was hypothesized as one of the original components of the controversial and mostly abandoned **Penutian** hypothesis.

witness   Attested linguistic form (sound, morpheme, word etc.) that is seen to exemplify proposed changes, reconstructions or etymologies. See also **attestation**.

word-order change   The study of word order and its implications for syntactic theory are the purview of the field of syntactic **typology**. The basic ordering of the core constituents of the simple, indicative sentence can change over time, as in the case of Latin SOV (Subject-Object-Verb) > **Romance** SVO (Subject-Verb-Object) ~ VSO (Verb-Subject-Object); **Indo-European** SOV (Subject-Object-Verb) > Celtic VSO. When not merely the result of contact with a **language** or languages with another word order, change can be motivated by constituent movement rules, such as topicalization, clefting, focus and so on, especially as what were once emphatic re-orderings become the normal order and the meaning becomes neutral. See also **mechanisms of syntactic change, synactic change**.

Wörter und Sachen (from German 'words and things') This is an analytic approach originally espoused by Jakob Grimm that allows for cultural inferences to be made on the basis of **historical linguistic** data, as is the case in **linguistic paleontology** or **linguistic prehistory**. The *Wörter und Sachen* movement was particularly influential in Germany, but has also played a significant role in historical linguistic work elsewhere, in particular as implemented by Edward Sapir and others in North America (see Sapir 1916). One technique favored in this approach is based on the criterion of the analyzability of words, by which greater structural opacity can be argued to correlate with greater age for the cultural referent whereas, morphological transparency or tractability can reflect recent coinage. Thus, in the geographic territory of a language, the more opaque toponyms can indicate an area of older settlement as opposed to those in which place names are more tractable, for example, *Paris, York, Coimbra, London, Zaragoza* as opposed to *Buenos Aires, Rio de Janeiro, Watertown, Portsmouth, Rapid City*. The situation is similar to that found in the original meaning of the *-ster* nominalizing suffix occurring in surnames like *Webster* 'weaver', *Baxter* 'baker', in which the occupational referent of *-ster* is still recoverable when compared to its productive use in other words (compare, for instance, *prankster, trickster, jokester*). An etymological analysis of the modern word, *spinster* 'an unmarried, usually older, woman', uncovers cultural data about the occupation, sex and marital status of the original practitioners of now-obsolescent art of spinning. In the Iberian peninsula the area occupied by the pre-Roman Celts is delimited in place names such as those with the Celtic element *briga* 'fortified settlement' (compare this with Germanic **burg*): *Betanzos* < **Brigantium, Coimbra* < **Conimbriga, Segorbe* < **Segobriga* (see **sego* 'victory' and German *Sieg* 'victory').

writing and language change   see **philology**

written evidence, written attestation   see **philology, writing and language change**

☒

Xinkan, Xincan   A small family of four languages of Guatemala, Chiquimulilla, Guazacapán, Jumaytepeque and Yupiltepeque. The first and last became extinct in the last two decades of the twentieth century; the other two have extremely few remaining speakers, only two or three each. Hypotheses have attempted to link Xinkan with various other languages in broader genetic groupings, but none has any value. The often repeated hypothesis of a connection between Xinkan and **Lencan** has no reliable evidence and is now abandoned.

Xinca-Lenca   Once proposed but now abandoned **distant genetic relationship** that sought to group the **Xinkan** and **Lencan** families. (See Campbell 1997: 961–3 for an evaluation.)

Y

Yeniseian, Yenisseian   Small **language family** of southern Siberia of which Ket (Khet) is the only surviving member. Yeniseian has no known broader relatives, though some have been hypothesized (see the **Dené-Caucasian** hypothesis).

Yokutsan   A family of some dozen languages of the San Joaquin Valley and adjacent areas of California. Yawelmani is perhaps the best known of several other varieties including Yachikumne, Chawchila and Wikchamni. Yokutsan was hypothesized as one of the original components of the controversial **Penutian** hypothesis.

Yuchi   A language **isolate**, spoken in eastern Tennessee in the sixteenth century with remaining speakers now in Georgia and Oklahoma. Yuchi has been hypothesized to belong together in a **distant genetic relationship** with **Siouan**, and the evidence for this relationship, if not conclusive, is quite suggestive.

Yukaghir   A small **language family** of Siberia, composed of

Tundra (Northern) Yukaghir and Kolyma (or Southern) Yukaghir. It is often thought possibly to be related to **Uralic**, though the evidence has not yet been sufficient to confirm this proposal.

Yukian   A small **language family** of northern California, made up of two branches, Wappo on the one hand and Yukian (with Yuki, Coast Yuki, and Huchnom) on the other.

Yuman   see **Cochimí-Yuman**

Z

zero-grade   see **ablaut**.

Zuni   A language **isolate** of New Mexico. None of the various attempts to classify Zuni with broader groups has had any success.

Bibliography

Adelaar, Willem F. (1989), 'Review of *Language in the Americas* by Joseph H. Greenberg', *Lingua*, 78: 249–55.

Andersen, Henning (1973), 'Abductive and Deductive Change', *Language*, 49: 765–93.

Andersen, Henning (1980), 'Morphological Change: Towards a Typology', in *Recent Developments in Historical Morphology*, Jacek Fisiak (ed.), The Hague: Mouton, pp. 1–50.

Anttila, Raimo (1972), *An Introduction to Historical and Comparative Linguistics*, New York: MacMillan, 1972 (2nd edn, 1989, *Current Issues in Linguistic Theory*, 4. Amsterdam: John Benjamins).

Beekes, Robert S. P. (1995), *Comparative Indo-European Linguistics: An Introduction*, Amsterdam: John Benjamins.

Benedict, Paul K. (1975), *Austro-Thai Language and Culture, with a Glossary of Roots*, New Haven, CT: Human Relations Area Files.

Benedict, Paul K. (1990), *Japanese/Austro-Tai*, Linguistica Extranea, Studia 20, Ann Arbor: Karoma Press.

Bengston, John (1991), 'Notes on Sino-Caucasian', in *Dene-Sino-Caucasian Languages: Materials from the First International Interdisciplinary Symposium on Language and Prehistory*, Vitaly Shevoroshkin (ed.), Bochum: Brockmeyer, pp. 67–15.

Bengston, John (1992), 'The Macro-Caucasian Phonology', *The Dene-Caucasian Macrophylum. Nostratic, Dene-Caucasian, Austric and Amerind: Materials from the First International Interdisciplinary Symposium on Language and Prehistory*, Vitaly Shevoroshkin (ed.), Bochum: Brockmeyer, pp. 342–51.

Bengston, John (1997), 'Basque and the other Dené-Caucasic Languages', *LACUS Forum*, 23: 137–48.

Bengston, John D. and Ruhler, Merritt (1994), 'Global Etymologies', in *On the Origin of Languages: Studies in Linguistic Taxonomy*, by Merritt Rihler, Stanford: Stanford University Press, pp. 237–336.

Bickerton, Derek (1985), *Roots of Language*, Ann Arbor: Karoma Press.

Blažek, V. and Bengston, John (1995), 'V. Lexica Dene-Caucasica', *Central Asiatic Journal*, 39: 11–50.

Bloch, Oscar and von Wartburg, Walther (1968), *Dictionnaire etymologique de la langue française*, 5th edn, Paris: Les Presses Universitaires de France.

Boas, Franz and Deloria, E.C. (1941), *Dakhota Grammar: Memoirs of the National Academy of Sciences*, vol. 23, Washington: US Government Printing Office.

Brown, Cecil H. and Witkowski, Stanley R. (1979), 'Aspects of the Phonological History of Mayan Zoquean', *International Journal of American Linguistics*, 45: 34–47.

Campbell, Lyle (1973), 'Distant Genetic Relationships and the Maya-Chipaya Hypothesis', *Anthropological Linguistics*, 15.3: 113–35. (Reprinted 1993, 'Special Issue: A Retrospective of the Journal of Anthropological Linguistics: selected papers, 1959–1985', *Anthropological Linguistics*, 35.1–4: 66–89.)

Campbell, Lyle (1988), 'Review of *Language in the Americas*, by Joseph Greenberg', *Language*, 64: 591–615.

Campbell, Lyle (1990), 'Syntactic Reconstruction and Finno-Ugric', in *Historical Linguistics 1987*, Henning Andersen and Konrad Koerner (eds), Amsterdam: John Benjamins, pp. 51–94.

Campbell, Lyle (1995), 'The Quechumaran Hypothesis and Lessons for Distant Genetic Comparison', *Diachronica*, 12: 157–200.

Campbell, Lyle (1997), *American Indian Languages: The Historical Linguistics of Native America*, Oxford: Oxford University Press.

Campbell, Lyle (1998), 'Nostratic: A Personal Assessment', in Brian Joseph and Joe Salmons (eds), *Nostratic: Sifting the Evidence*, Amsterdam: John Benjamins, pp. 107–52.

Campbell, Lyle (1999), 'Nostratic and Linguistic Palaeontology in Methodological Perspective', in Colin Renfrew and Daniel Nettle (eds), *Nostratic: Evaluating a Linguistic Macrofamily*, Cambridge: The McDonald Institute for Archaeological Research, pp. 179–230.

Campbell, Lyle (2003), 'How to Show Languages are Related: Methods for Distant Genetic Relationship', in Brian D. Joseph and Richard D. Janda (eds), *Handbook of Historical Linguistics*, Oxford: Blackwell, pp. 262–82.

Campbell, Lyle (2004), *Historical Linguistics: An Introduction*, 2nd edn, Edinburgh: Edinburgh University Press.

Campbell, Lyle and Kaufman, Terrence (1976), 'A Linguistic Look at the Olmecs', *American Antiquity*, 41: 80–9.

Campbell, Lyle, Kaufman, Terrence and Smith-Stark, Thomas (1986), 'Mesoamerica as a Linguistic Area', *Language*, 62: 530–70.

Campbell, Lyle and Poser, William (in press), *Language Classification:*

History and Method, Cambridge: Cambridge University Press.

Campbell, Lyle and Ringen, Jon (1981), 'Teleology and the Explanation of Sound Change', in *Phonologica*, Wolfgang U. Dressler, Oskar E. Pfeiffer and John R. Rennison (eds), Innsbruck: Innsbrucker Beiträge zur Sprachwissenschaft, pp. 57–68.

Chafe, Wallace (1976), *The Caddoan, Iroquoian, and Siouan Languages,* The Hague: Mouton.

Chen, Matthew Y. and Wang, William S.-Y. (1975), 'Sound Change: Actuation and Implementation', *Language,* 51: 255–81.

Collinge, N. E. (1985), *The Laws of Indo-European,* Amsterdam: John Benjamins.

Corominas, Joan (1974), *Diccionario crítico etimológico de la lengua castellana,* 4 vols, Madrid: Gredos.

Corominas, Juan and Pascual, José (1980), *Diccionario etimológico castellano e hispánico,* Madrid: Gredos.

Cortelazzo, Manlio and Zolli, Paolo (1979–1988), *Dizionario etimologico della lingua italiana,* Bologna: Zanichelli.

Crowley, Terry (1997), *An Introduction to Historical Linguistics,* 3rd edn, Auckland: Oxford University Press.

de Reuse, Willem J. (1994). *Siberian Yupik Eskimo: The Language and its Contacts with Chukchi,* Salt Lake City: University of Utah Press.

Delbrück, Berthold (1878), *Syntaktische Forschungen, III.* Halle: Niemeyer.

Derbyshire, Desmond C. and Payne, Doris L. (1990), 'Noun Classification Systems of Amazonian Languages', *Amazonian Linguistics: Studies in Lowland South American Languages,* Doris L. Payne (ed.), Austin: University of Texas Press, pp. 243–71.

Derbyshire, Desmond C. and Pullum, Geoffrey K. (1986), 'Introduction', *Handbook of Amazonian Languages,* vol. 1, Desmond C. Derbyshire and Geoffrey K. Pullum (eds), Berlin: Mouton de Gruyter, pp. 1–28.

Dixon, R. M. W. (1997), *The Rise and Fall of Languages,* Cambridge: Cambridge University Press.

Dixon, R. M. W. (2002), *Australian Languages,* Cambridge: Cambridge University Press.

Dixon, R. M. W. and Aikhenvald, Alexandra Y. (1999), 'Introduction', *The Amazonian Languages,* R. M. W. Dixon and Alexandra Y. Aikhenvald (eds), Cambridge: Cambridge University Press, pp. 1–21.

Dixon, Roland and Kroeber, Alfred L. (1913a), 'New Linguistic Families in California', *American Anthropologist,* 15: 647–55.

Dixon, Roland and Kroeber, Alfred L. (1913b), 'Relationship of the Indian Languages of California', *Science,* 37: 225.

Dixon, Roland and Kroeber, Alfred L. (1919), 'Linguistic Families of California', *University of California Publications in American Archaeology and Ethnology* no. 16, 47–118, Berkeley: University of California.

Embleton, Sheila M. (1986), *Statistics in Historical Linguistics,* Bochum: Brockmeyer.

Emeneau, Murray B. (1956), 'India as a Linguistic Area', *Language* 32: 3–16.

Emeneau, Murray B. (1980), *Language and Linguistic Area, Essays by Murray B. Emeneau,* selected and introduced by Anwar S. Dil, Stanford: Stanford University Press.

Ferguson, Charles (1976), 'The Ethiopian Language Area', in *Language in Ethiopia,* M. L. Bender, J. D. Bowen, R. L. Cooper and C. A. Ferguson (eds), Oxford: Oxford University Press, pp. 63–76.

Finck, Franz Nikolaus (1909), *Die Sprachstämme des Erdkreises,* Leipzig: B. G. Teubner.

Fishman, Joshua A. (1991), *Reversing Language Shift: Theoretical and Empirical Foundations of Assistance to Threatened Languages,* Multilingual Matters.

Foley, William (2000), 'The Languages of New Guinea', *Annual Review of Anthropology,* 29: 357–404.

Gamkrelidze, T. V. and Ivanov, V. V. (1973), 'Sprachtypologie und die Rekonstruktion der gemeinindogermanischen Verschlüsse', *Phonetica,* 27: 150–6.

Georg, Stefan and Vovin, Alexander (2003), 'From Mass Comparison to Mess Comparison: Greenberg's *Indo-European and its Closest Relatives*' (review article), *Diachronica,* 20: 331–62.

Georg, Stefan and Vovin, Alexander (2005), 'Review of *Indo-European and its Closest Relatives: The Eurasiatic Language Family, vol. 2: The Lexicon*', by Joseph H. Greenberg, *Diachronica,* 22: 184–90.

Gilliéron, Jules (1921), *Pathologie et thérapeutique verbales,* Paris: Champion.

Gilliéron, Jules and Roques, Mario (1912), *Études de géographie linguistique,* Paris: Champion.

Gimbutas, Marija (1963), 'The Indo-Europeans: Archaeological Problems', *American Antrhopologist,* 65: 815–36.

Givón, Talmy (1990), 'Syntax: A Functional–Typological Introduction', vol. 2, Amsterdam: John Benjamins.

Gordon, Elizabeth, Campbell, Lyle, Hay, Jennifer, Maclagan, Margaret, Sudbury, Andrea and Trudgill, Peter (2004), *New Zealand English: Its Origins and Evolution,* Cambridge: Cambridge University Press.

Greenberg, Joseph H. (1963), *Languages of Africa,* Bloomington: Indiana University Publications of the Research Center in Anthropology, Folklore, and Linguistics, no. 25.

Greenberg, Joseph H. (1971), *The Indo-Pacific Hypothesis. Current Trends in Linguistics, 8: Linguistics in Oceania*, Thomas A. Sebeok (ed.), The Hague: Mouton, pp. 807–71.

Greenberg, Joseph H. (1987), *Language in the Americas*, Stanford: Stanford University. Press.

Greenberg, Joseph H. (2000), *Indo-European and its Closest Relatives: The Eurasiatic Language Family*, Stanford: Stanford University Press.

Greenberg, Joseph H. (2002), *Indo-European and its Closest Relatives: The Eurasiatic Language Family, vol. 2: The Lexicon*, Stanford: Stanford University Press.

Gudschinsky, Sarah (1956), 'The ABC's of Lexicostatistics (Glottochronology)', *Word*, 12: 175–210.

Haas, Mary R. (1951), 'The Proto-Gulf Word for *Water* (With Notes on Siouan-Yuchi)', *International Journal of American Linguistics*, 17: 71–9.

Haas, Mary R. (1952), The Proto-Gulf Word for *Land* (With notes on Siouan-Yuchi), *International Journal of American Linguistics*, 18: 238–40.

Haas, Mary R. (1958a), 'Algonkian-Ritwan: The End of a Controversy', *International Journal of American Linguistics*, 24: 159–73.

Haas, Mary R. (1958b), 'A New Linguistic Relationship in North America: Algonkian and the Gulf Languages', *Southwestern Journal of Anthropology*, 14: 231–64.

Haas, Mary R. (1960), 'Some Genetic Affiliations of Algonkian', in *Culture in History: Essays in Honor of Paul Radin*, Stanley Diamond (ed.), New York: Columbia University Press, pp. 977–92.

Haiman, John (1979), 'Hua: A Papuan Language of New Guinea', *Languages and Their Status*, Timothy Shopen (ed.), Philadelphia: University of Pennsylvania Press, pp. 35–89.

Harris, Alice C. and Campbell, Lyle (1995), *Historical Syntax in Cross-Linguistic Perspective*, Cambridge: Cambridge University Press.

Heine, Bernd and Reh, Mechthild (1984), *Grammaticalisation and Reanalysis in African Languages*, Hamburg: Buske.

Hinton, Leanne and Hale, Ken (eds) (2001), *The Green Book of Language Revitalization and Practice*, San Diego, San Francisco, New York: Academic Press.

Hogg, Richard M. (1992), 'Phonology and Morphology', *The Cambridge History of the English Language, Vol. 1: The Beginnings to 1066*, Richard Hogg (ed.), Cambridge: Cambridge University Press, pp. 67–167.

Hopper, Paul J. (1973), 'Glottalized and Murmured Occlusives in Indo-European', *Glossa*, 7: 141–66.

Hopper, Paul J. and Closs Traugott, Elizabeth (1993), *Grammaticalization*, Cambridge: Cambridge University Press.

Jakobson, Roman (1931), 'Prinzipien der historischen Phonologie', *Travaux du Cercle Linguistique de Prague*, 4: 247–67.

Kaiser, Mark and Shevoroshkin. Vitaly (1988), 'Nostratic', *Annual Review of Anthropology*, 17: 309–30.

Kaufman, Terrence (1990), 'Language History in South America: What We Know and How to Know More', in *Amazonian Linguistics: Studies in Lowland South American Languages*, Doris L. Payne (ed.), Austin: University of Texas Press, pp. 13–67.

Kaufman, Terrence (1994), 'The Native Languages of South America', in *Atlas of the World's Languages*, Christopher Moseley and R. E. Asher (eds), London: Routledge, pp. 46–76.

Keller, Rudi (1994), *On Language Change: The Invisible Hand in Language*, London: Routledge.

Kimball, Geoffrey (1992), 'A Critique of Muskogean, "Gulf", and Yukian Material', in *Language in the Americas. International Journal of American Linguistics*, 58: 447–501.

Kluge, Friedrich (1975), *Etymologisches Wörterbuch der deutschen Sprache*, 21st edn (1st edn 1883), Berlin: De Gruyter.

Koptjevskaja-Tamm, Maria and Wälchli, Bernhard (2001), 'The Circum-Baltic Languages: An Areal-Typological Approach', in *The Circum-Baltic Languages: Typology and Contact*, Östen Dahl and Maria Koptjevskaja-Tamm (eds), Amsterdam: John Benjamins, pp. 615–761.

Kurlowicz, Jerzy (2001), 'The Evolution of Grammatical Categories', *Diogenes*, 1965, 51: 55–71.

Labov, William (1994), *Principles of Linguistic Change: Internal Factors*, Oxford: Blackwell.

Lass, Roger (1990), 'Where do Extraterritorial Englishes Come From? Dialect Input and Recodification in Transported Englishes', *Papers from the Fifth International Conference on English Historical Linguistics*, S. Adamson, V. Law, N. Vincent and S. Wright (eds), pp. 245–80.

Lehmann, Christian (2002), 'New Reflections on Grammaticalization and Lexicalization', in *New Reflections on Grammaticalization*, Ilse Wischer and Gabriele Diewald (eds), Amsterdam: John Benjamins, pp. 1–18.

McAlpin, David W. (1974), 'Toward Proto-Elamo-Dravidian Language', *Language*, 50: 89–101.

McAlpin, David W. (1981), Proto-Elamo-Dravidian: The Evidence and

Implications', *Transactions of the American Philosophical Society*, vol. 71, part 3, Philadelphia: American Philosophical Society.

McMahon, April and McMahon, R. (1995), 'Linguistics, Genetics and Archaeology: Internal and External Evidence in the Amerind Controversy', *Transactions of the Philological Society*, 93: 125–225.

Martinet, André (1970), *Économie des changements phonétiques: traité de phonologie diachronique*, 3rd edn (1st edn 1955), Berne: A. Francke.

Masica, Colin P. (1976), *Defining a Linguistic Area: South Asia*, Chicago: University of Chicago Press.

Masica, Colin P. (1991), *The Indo-Aryan Languages*, Cambridge: Cambridge University Press.

Matthews, P. H. (1997), *The Concise Oxford Dictionary of Linguistics*, Oxford: Oxford University Press.

Meillet, Antoine (1912), 'L'Évolution des formes grammaticales', *Scientia*, 12/26, Milan. (Reprinted 1951, *Linguistique historique et linguistique générale*, Paris: C. Klincksieck, pp. 130–48.)

Miller, Wick R. (1959), 'A Note on Kiowa Linguistic Affiliations', *American Anthropologist*, 61: 102–5.

Miller, Wick R. (1983), Uto-Aztecan Languages', in *Southwest*, Alonso Ortiz (ed.), vol. 10 of *Handbook of North American Indians*, ed. William C. Sturetevant, Washington, DC: Smithsonian Institution, pp. 113–24

Milroy, James (1992), *Linguistic Variation and Change: On the Historical Sociolinguistics of English,* Oxford: Blackwell.

Mixco, Mauricio J. (1977), 'The Linguistic Response of Kiliwa to Hispanic Culture', *Proceedings of the Third Annual Meeting of the Berkeley Linguistics Society*, Berkeley: Berkeley Linguistics Society, pp. 24–37.

Mixco, Mauricio J. (1983), 'Kiliwa Texts', *Anthropological Papers*, 107, Salt Lake City: University of Utah Press.

Mixco, Mauricio J. (1985), 'Kiliwa Dictionary', *Anthropological Papers*, 109, Salt Lake City: University of Utah Press.

Mixco, Mauricio J. (1997), 'Haas's Hokan: Dead End, or Gateway to the Future?' *Anthropological Linguistics*, 39 (4): 629–35.

Mixco, Mauricio J. (2000a), *'Kiliwa del Arroyo del León de la Baja California Norte'*, *Archivo de Lenguas Indígenas de México. Vol. 18*, Yolanda Lastra (ed.), Mexico, DF: UNAM/El Colegio de México Presses.

Mixco, Mauricio J. (2000b), *'Sketch of Kiliwa Grammar'*, *Languages of the World Series*, Unterschleissheim (Munich): LINCOM EUROPA.

Moreno Cabrera, Juan C. (1998), 'On the Relationship between

Grammaticalization and Lexicalization', *The Limits of Grammaticalization*, Anna Giacalone and Paul Hopper (eds), Amsterdam: John Benjamins, pp. 209–27.

Mufwene, Salikoko S. (2001), *The Ecology of Language Evolution*, Cambridge: Cambridge University Press.

Mutaka, Ngessimo N. (2000), *An Introduction to African Linguistics*, Munich: LINCOM Europa.

Newman, Paul (2000), 'Comparative Linguistics' in *African Languages: An Introduction*, Bernd Heine and Derek Nurse (eds), Cambridge: Cambridge University Press, pp. 259–71.

Nichols, Johanna (1990), 'Linguistic Diversity and the First Settlement of the New World', *Language*, 66: 475–521.

Nichols, Johanna (1992), *Linguistic Diversity in Time and Space*, Chicago: University of Chicago Press.

Nichols, Johanna (1997), 'Modeling Ancient Population Structures and Movement in Linguistics', *Annual Review of Anthropology*, 26: 359–84.

Nurse, Derek (1997), 'The Contributions of Linguistics to the Study of History in Africa', *Journal of African History*, 38: 359–91.

Olson, Ronald D. (1964), 'Mayan Affinities with Chipaya of Bolivia I: Correspondences', *International Journal of American Linguistics*, 30: 313–24.

Olson, Ronald D. (1965), 'Mayan Affinities with Chipaya of Bolivia II: Cognates', *International Journal of American Linguistics*, 31: 29–38.

Osthoff, Hermann and Brugmann, Karl (1878), *Morphologische Untersuchungen auf dem Gebiete der indogermanischen Sprachen*, Leipzig: S. Hirzel.

Pokorny, Julius, *Indogermanisches etymologisches Wörterbuch*, Bern: Francke.

Poser, William J. (1992), 'The Salinan and Yurumanguí Data', *Language in the Americas: International Journal of American Linguistics*, 58: 202–29.

Rankin, Robert L. (1992), 'Review of *Language in the Americas*, by Joseph H. Greenberg', *International Journal of American Linguistics*, 58: 324–51.

Renfrew, Colin (1996), 'Language Families and the Spread of Farming', in *The Origins and Spread of Agriculture and Pastoralism in Eurasia*, D. R. Harris (ed.), London: University College London Press, pp. 70–92.

Ringe, Donald A., Jr. (1992), 'On Calculating the Factor of Chance in Language Comparison', *Transactions of the American Philosophical Society*, 82.1: 1–110.

Ringe, Donald A., Jr. (1996), 'The Mathematics of "Amerind"',

Diachronica, 13: 135–54.

Rodrigues, Aryon (1986), *Linguas brasileiras: para o conhecimento das linguas indígenas*, São Paulo: Edições Loyola.

Romaine, Suzanne (1982), *Socio-historical Linguistics: Its Status and Methodology*, Cambridge: Cambridge University Press.

Ross, Malcolm D. (1996), 'Contact-induced Change and the Comparative Method: Cases from Papua New Guinea', *The Comparative Method Reviewed: Regularity and Irregularity in Language Change*, Mark Durie and Malcolm Ross (eds), Oxford: Oxford University Press, pp. 180–217.

Ross, Malcolm D. (1997), 'Social Networks and Kinds of Speech Community Events', *Archaeology and Language, 1: Theoretical and Methodological Orientations*, R. M. Blench and Matthew Spriggs (eds), London: Routledge, pp. 209–16.

Sapir, Edward (1913), 'Wiyot and Yurok, Algonkin Languages of California', *American Anthropologist*, 15: 617–46.

Sapir, Edward (1915), 'The Na-Dené Languages, a Preliminary Report', *American Anthropologist*, 17: 534–58.

Sapir, Edward (1916), 'Time Perspective in Aboriginal American Culture: A Study in Method'. Department of Mines, Geological Survey, Memoir No. 90. Ottawa: Government Printing Bureau. (Reprinted 1949 as *Selected Writings of Edward Sapir in Language, Culture, and Personality*, David G. Mandelbaum (ed.), Berkeley: University of California Press, pp. 389–467.)

Sapir, Edward (1920), 'The Hokan and Coahuiltecan Languages', *International Journal of American Linguistics*, 1: 280–90.

Sapir, Edward (1921), *Language: An Introduction to the Study of Speech*, New York: Harcourt, Brace and World.

Sapir, Edward (1925), 'The Hokan Affinity of Subtiaba in Nicaragua', *American Anthropologist*, 27: 402–35, 491–527.

Sapir, Edward (1929), 'Central and North American Languages', *Encyclopaedia Britannica*, 14th edn, 5: 138–41. (Reprinted 1949, *Selected Writings of Edward Sapir in Language, Culture, and Personality*, David G. Mandelbaum (ed.), Berkeley: University of California Press, pp. 169–78.)

Schmidt, Wilhelm (1906), 'Die Mon-Khmer-Völker, ein Bindeglied zwischen Völkern Zentralasiens und Austronesiens', *Archiv für Anthropologie*, 33: 59–109.

Schuchardt, Hugo (1868), *Das Vokalismus des Vulgärlateins*, vol. 3, Leipzig: B. G. Teubner.

Shevoroshkin, Vitaly (1991), 'Introduction', in *Dene-Sino-Caucasian Languages: Materials from the First International Interdisciplinary Symposium on Language and Prehistory*, Vitaly Shevoroshkin (ed.),

Bochum: Brockmeyer, pp. 6–9.

Stark, Louisa R. (1970), 'Mayan Affinities with Araucanian', *Chicago Linguistics Society*, 6: 57–69.

Stark, Louisa R. (1972), 'Maya-Yunga-Chipayan: A New Linguistic Alignment', *International Journal of American Linguistics*, 38: 119–35.

Sturtevant, Edgar (1917), *Linguistic Change: An Introduction to the Historical Study of Language*, Chicago: The University of Chicago Press.

Swadesh, Morris (1953a), 'Mosan I: A Problem of Remote Common Origin', *International Journal of American Linguistics*, 19: 26–44.

Swadesh, Morris (1953b), 'Mosan II: Comparative Vocabulary', *International Journal of American Linguistics*, 19: 223–36.

Thomason, Sarah G. (2001), *Language Contact: An Introduction*, Edinburgh: Edinburgh University Press.

Thomason, Sarah Grey and Kaufman, Terrence (1988), *Language Contact, Creolization, and Genetic Linguistics*, Berkeley: University of California Press.

Thurston, W. R. (1989), 'How Exoteric Languages Build a Lexicon', in *VICAL 1: Oceanic languages: Papers of the 5th International Conference of Austronesian Linguistics*, Ray Harlow and Robin Hooper (eds), Auckland: Linguistic Society of New Zealand, pp. 555–80.

Tosco, Mauro (2000), 'Is there an "Ethiopian Language Area"?' *Antrhopological Linguistics*, 42: 329–65.

Trask, R. L. (1996), *Historical Linguistics*, London: Arnold.

Trask, R. L. (2000), *The Dictionary of Historical and Comparative Linguistics*, Edinburgh: Edinburgh University Press.

Trudgill, Peter (1986), *Dialects in Contact*, Oxford: Blackwell.

Van Driem, George (2001), *Languages of the Himalayas*, 2 vols, Leiden: Brill.

Wang, William (1969), 'Competing Sound Changes as a Cause of Residue', *Language*, 45: 9–25.

Wartburg, Walther von (1922), *Französisches Etymologisches Wörterbuch*, Bonn: F. Klopp.

Watkins, Calvert (1962), *Indo-European Origins of the Celtic Verb I: The Sigmatic Aorist*, Dublin: Dublin Institute for Advanced Studies.

Weinreich, Uriel, Labov, William and Herzog, Marvin (1968), 'Empirical Foundations for a Theory of Language Change', *Directions for Historical Linguistics*, Austin: University of Texas Press, pp. 95–195.

Wessén, Elias (1969), *Språkhistoria I: ljudlära och ordböjningslära*, Stockholm: Almqvist & Wiksell.

Whorf, Benjamin L. and George L. Trager (1937), 'The Relationship of Uto-Aztecan and Tanoan', *American Anthropologist*, 39: 609–24.

Wischer, Ilse (2000), 'Grammaticalization versus Lexicalization: "Methinks" There is Some Confussion', *Pathways of Change: Grammaticalization in English*, O. Fischer, A. Rosenbach and D. Stein (eds), Amsterdam: John Benjamins, pp. 355–70.

Zeps, Valdis (1962), *Latvian and Finnic Linguistic Convergence*, Uralic and Altaic Series, No. 9, Bloomington: Indiana University Press.